THE LAND
GOVERNANCE
ASSESSMENT
FRAMEWORK

AGRICULTURE AND RURAL DEVELOPMENT

Seventy-five percent of the world's poor live in rural areas and most are involved in agriculture. In the 21st century, agriculture remains fundamental to economic growth, poverty alleviation, and environmental sustainability. The World Bank's Agriculture and Rural Development publication series presents recent analyses of issues that affect the role of agriculture, including livestock, fisheries, and forestry, as a source of economic development, rural livelihoods, and environmental services. The series is intended for practical application, and we hope that it will serve to inform public discussion, policy formulation, and development planning.

Titles in this series:

THE LAND
GOVERNANCE
ASSESSMENT
FRAMEWORK

Identifying and Monitoring Good Practice in the Land Sector

Klaus Deininger, Harris Selod, and Anthony Burns

THE WORLD BANK
Washington, D.C.

This volume is a product of the staff of the International Bank for Reconstruction and Development/The World Bank. The findings, interpretations, and conclusions expressed in this volume do not necessarily reflect the views of the Executive Directors of The World Bank or the governments they represent.

The World Bank does not guarantee the accuracy of the data included in this work. The boundaries, colors, denominations, and other information shown on any map in this work do not imply any judgement on the part of The World Bank concerning the legal status of any territory or the endorsement or acceptance of such boundaries.

Rights and Permissions

ISBN: 978-0-8213-8758-0
eISBN: 978-0-8213-8759-7
DOI: 10.1596/978-0-8213-8758-0
ISSN: None

Library of Congress Cataloging-in-Publication Data
Deininger, Klaus W., 1962-
  The land governance assessment framework: identifying and monitoring good practice in the land sector / Klaus Deininger, Harris Selod, and Anthony Burns.
    p. cm. — (Agriculture and rural development)
  Includes bibliographical references.
  ISBN 978-0-8213-8758-0 — ISBN 978-0-8213-8759-7 (electronic)
  1. Land use, Rural, 2. Land tenure. 3. Public lands—Management. I. Selod, Harris. II. Burns, Anthony (Anthony F.) III. World Bank. IV. Title.
  HD111.D357 2012
  333.73—dc23

                                                                    2011037612

Cover photo: Klaus Deininger
Cover design: Critical Stages

CONTENTS

BOXES AND TABLES

Boxes

Tables

ABOUT THE AUTHORS

Klaus Deininger is the lead economist in the World Bank's Development Research Group. His research focuses on inequality and its impact on poverty reduction and growth; on the impact of land access, tenure, and reform on household welfare and agricultural productivity; on the political economy of decentralized rural development; and on impact evaluation and capacity building in developing countries. For the past four years, he has also been the World Bank's land tenure adviser. He holds a Ph.D. in applied economics from the University of Minnesota and has published more than 50 articles and a number of books, including a 2003 report, "Land Policies for Growth and Poverty Reduction," and a recent book, *Rising Global Interest in Farmland: Can It Yield Sustainable and Equitable Benefits?*

Harris Selod is a senior economist with the Development Research Group of the World Bank, Land Policy and Administration Thematic Group. His research focuses on land governance; land markets; and the spatial organization of rural, urban, and peri-urban areas in developing countries, with a specific interest in West Africa. His publications cover a number of topics in regional and public economics, including theories of squatting and residential informality, the political economy of investments in transport infrastructure, the effects of residential segregation on schooling and unemployment, and the impact of land rights formalization and place-based policies. He is a coauthor of *Rising Global Interest in Farmland: Can It Yield Sustainable and Equitable Benefits?* Prior to joining the World Bank in 2007, he was an associate professor at the Paris

School of Economics and a researcher at the French National Institute for Agricultural Research. He holds a Ph.D. in economics from the University of Paris Panthéon-Sorbonne and degrees in statistics from the Ecole Nationale de la Statistique et de l'Administration Economique and in business administration from the Ecole Supérieure de Commerce de Paris.

Tony Burns is a land administration specialist with extensive experience in designing, managing, and evaluating systematic registration and land administration projects. He is the managing director of Land Equity International, a company focused on supporting land administration projects worldwide. He has more than 25 years of experience on land sector projects, including experience as a team leader and project director, supervising large-scale, long-term, multidisciplinary projects. He has also undertaken numerous short-term consultancies for a range of multilateral and bilateral development partners. His technical expertise includes land policy, cadastral survey and mapping, systematic registration, land administration, and spatial information systems.

ACKNOWLEDGMENTS

The Land Governance Assessment Framework (LGAF) is a diagnostic tool to help evaluate the legal framework, policies, and practices regarding land governance and to monitor improvement over time. It emerged from a collaborative process between the World Bank and its partners that was based on the recognition of the increasingly important role of land governance to help countries deal with the challenges of the 21st century in terms of climate change, urbanization, disaster prevention, and management of increased demand for land in an integrated way that provides a basis for demonstrating progress over time.

The process of designing the LGAF benefited tremendously from the experience of and interaction with other land governance initiatives, including the Legal and Institutional Framework Index of the United Nations Human Settlements Programme (UN-Habitat); the Blueprint for Strengthening Real Property Rights of the United States Agency for International Development and the Inter American Alliance; the ongoing process by the Food and Agriculture Organization of the United Nations (FAO) to establish Voluntary Guidelines for Responsible Governance of Tenure of Land and Other Natural Resources; and the Framework and Guidelines on Land Policy recently developed under the leadership of the African Union, the United Nations Economic Commission for Africa (UNECA), and the African Development Bank.

The LGAF was developed by a team led by Klaus Deininger and comprising Harris Selod and Daniel Monchuk (World Bank) and Tony Burns and Kate Dalrymple (Land Equity International), following up on an initiative by Wael Zakout and in close collaboration with the World Bank's thematic group on land policy and administration, the African Union Land Policy Initiative, the FAO, the International Fund for Agricultural Development (IFAD), and UN-Habitat. The guidance, support, and leadership of management in the World Bank's Agriculture and Development Department, in particular, Juergen Voegele and Mark Cackler, and in the World Bank's Development Economics Research Group, in particular, Martin Ravallion and Will Martin, was critical for developing the LGAF. Country pilots in Ethiopia, Indonesia, the Kyrgyz Republic, Peru, and Tanzania, led by Imeru Tamrat, Tristam Moelinio, Asyl Undeland, Victor Endo, and Lusugga Kironde, respectively, provided key input into the design and refinement of the instrument.

The study benefited from invaluable comments and suggestions made by peer reviewers Clarissa Augustinus (UN-Habitat); Paul Mathieu (FAO); Jolyne Sanjak and Jennifer Witriol (Millennium Challenge Corporation, MCC); Willi Zimmerman (Deutsche Gesellschaft für Internationale Zusammenarbeit); and Malcolm Childress, Nalin Kishor, Jonathan Lindsay, Una Meades, Stephen Mink, Eduardo Mosqueira, and Jorge Munoz (World Bank). In addition, invaluable insights were gained from technical and conceptual discussions and support from World Bank colleagues, including Gavin Adlington, Menberu Allebachew, Rachel Beach, Keith Bell, Derek Byerlee, Frank Byamugisha, Diji Chandrasekharan Behr, Edward Cook, Achim Fock, Madhur Gautam, Li Guo, Gloria Kessler, Nalin Kishor, Edgardo Maravi, Barjor Mehta, Jessica Mott, Andrew Norton, Kofi Nouve, Nuria de Oca, Maria Olavarria, Janelle Plummer, Robin Rajak, Michele Rebosio, Cora Shaw, Mercedes Stickler, Victoria Stanley, Andre Teyssier, Mika Thoronen (FAO), Jean-Philippe Tré, and David Varela. We are deeply indebted to many colleagues for their suggestions and comments and for their support throughout.

Key inputs were also obtained from Alain Durand-Lasserve (Centre National de la Recherche Scientifique), Regina Birner (International Food Policy Research Institute), Peter Adeniyi (University of Lagos, Department of Geography), John Bugri (Kwame Nkrumah University of Science and Technology), David Egiashvili, (Professional Consulting Group), Paul Jere (consultant), Mark Napier (Urban LandMark), Lionel Galliez (French Council of Notaries), Wily Giacchino (French Council of Notaries), Solomon Haile (UN-Habitat), Thea Hilhorst (Royal Tropical Institute), Joan Kagwanja (UNECA and Alliance for a Green Revolution in Africa), Olga Kaganova (Urban Institute), Annie Kairaba (Rwanda Initiative for Sustainable Development), Harold Liversage (IFAD), Annalisa Mauro (International Land Coalition [ILC]), Ruth Meinzen-Dick (IFPRI), Paul Munro-Faure (FAO), Patrick McAuslan (Birkbek College), Paul Nankivell (PDP Australia), Madiodio Niasse (ILC), Hubert Ouedraogo (UNECA), Vatche Papazian (Agence Francaise de Developpement), Tanja Pickardt (Deutsche Gesellschaft für Internationale Zusammenarbeit), Caroline Plançon (French Ministry of Foreign Affairs), Geir Sundet (Daylight Initiatives Norway), Rémy Sietchiping (UN-Habitat), Michael Taylor (ILC), Jose Tonato (Impact Consultants), Frits van der

Wal (Dutch Ministry for Foreign Affairs), and Lionel Vignac (French Ministry of Foreign Affairs), and Babette Wehrmann.

Numerous individuals provided feedback and support to developing the LGAF at a number of workshops and events, including a workshop surrounding the 13th International Anti-Corruption Conference organized by Transparency International in Athens in 2008; the 2008 and 2009 World Bank Annual Land Conferences in Washington, D.C.; regional consultations of the FAO's Voluntary Guidelines for Responsible Governance of Tenure of Land and Other Natural Resources held throughout 2009–10 in Addis Ababa, Budapest, Hanoi, London, and Ouagadougou; and the 2010 FIG Congress in Sydney. We acknowledge financial support provided by the Norwegian Governance Trust Fund and the Swiss Agency for Development and Cooperation, the Bill and Melinda Gates Foundation, the Global Land Tool Network, the William and Flora Hewitt Foundation, and the Omidyar Network. We also thank the French Ministry of Foreign Affairs for helping fund forthcoming LGAFs in a selection of francophone African countries.

Use of the LGAF as a diagnostic tool is being expanded through a land governance monitoring and assessment partnership involving as its founding partners, IFPRI, UN-Habitat, IFAD, FAO, and the World Bank. It is hoped that the combined expertise of these partners and others who are likely to join will ensure that the framework developed here will help to diagnose land policies, monitor progress in implementing pro-poor and gender sensitive approaches, and point toward global best practice, thereby not only responding to countries' and partners' needs for monitoring in this area, but also providing a basis for more sustained support to the land sector through a range of new instruments that depend on more rigorous monitoring.

ABBREVIATIONS

BAL	Basic Agrarian Law (Indonesia)
BPHTB	Bea Pengalihan Hak Atas Tanah Dan Bangunan
BPN	Badan Pertanahan Nasional (Indonesian National Land Agency)
CCRO	Certificate of Customary Right of Occupancy (Tanzania)
COFOPRI	Commission for the Formalization of Informal Property
CPIA	Country Policy and Institutional Assessment
CRO	Certificate of Right of Occupancy
CVL	Certificate of Village Land (Tanzania)
FAO	Food and Agriculture Organization of the United Nations
ha	Hectare
HGB	*Hak Guna Bangunan*
IBC	Institute for Well-Being (Peru)
IDA	International Development Association
IFAD	International Fund for Agricultural Development
LA	Land Act (Tanzania)
LGAF	Land Governance Assessment Framework
LGI	Land Governance Indicators
LIFI	Legal and Institutional Framework Index
LRF	Land Redistribution Fund (Kyrgyz Republic)
MKURABITA	Formalization Program in Tanzania (Masilimali na Biashara za Wanyonge Tanzania umeanzishwa na Serikali ya Jamhuri ya Muungano wa Tanzania)
PEFA	Public Expenditure and Financial Accountability

RC	Registered Condominium
RL	Residential License
SNNP	Southern Nations, Nationalities, and Peoples
s.t.	Strata Title (condominium)
SUNARP	National Superintendency of Public Registries (Peru)
VLA	Village Land Act (Tanzania)

BACKGROUND AND MOTIVATION

Increased global demand for land because of higher and more volatile food prices, urbanization, and use of land for environmental services implies an increased need for well-designed land policies at the country level to ensure security of long-held rights, to facilitate land access, and to deal with externalities. Establishing the infrastructure necessary to proactively deal with these challenges can require large amounts of resources. Yet with land tenure deeply rooted in any country's history, a wide continuum of land rights, and vast differences in the level of socioeconomic development, the benefits to be expected and the challenges faced will vary across and even within countries, implying a need to adapt the nature and sequencing of reforms to country circumstances. Also, as reforms will take time to bear fruit and may be opposed by vested interests, there is a need to identify challenges and to reach consensus on how to address them in a way that allows objective monitoring of progress over time. Without this being done, the chances of making quick progress in addressing key land policy challenges are likely to be much reduced.

The Land Governance Assessment Framework (LGAF) is intended as a first step to help countries deal with these issues. It is a diagnostic tool that is to be implemented at the local level in a collaborative fashion, that addresses the need for guidance to diagnose and benchmark land governance, and that can help countries prioritize reforms and monitor progress over time. The core version of the LGAF comprises a set of detailed indicators to be rated on a scale of precoded statements (from lack of good governance to good practice) based, where possible, on existing information. These indicators are grouped within five broad thematic areas that have been identified as major areas for policy intervention in the land sector:

- *Legal and institutional framework.* Indicators related to the legal and institutional framework are designed to help policy makers assess (a) the extent to which the range of existing land rights is legally recognized, (b) the level of documentation and enforcement, the cost of enforcing or gradually upgrading these rights, and (c) whether regulation and management of land involve institutions with clear mandates as well as policy processes that are transparent and equitable.
- *Land use planning, management, and taxation.* The intention of this category is to assess whether (a) land use restrictions are justified on the basis of the public interest, (b) necessary exemptions are granted promptly and transparently, (c) the process for land use planning is efficient, and (d) taxes on land and real estate are transparently determined and efficiently collected.
- *Management of public land.* A focus on public land management aims to help assess the extent to which (a) public landholdings are justified and transparently inventoried and managed; (b) expropriation procedures are applied in the public interest through clear, transparent, and fair processes involving the compensation of all those who lose rights; and (c) the transfer or devolution of state land is transparent and monitored.
- *Public provision of land information.* Indicators related to this category assess (a) whether land information systems provide sufficient, relevant, and up-to-date data on land ownership to the general public and (b) whether land administration services are accessible, affordable, and sustainable.
- *Dispute resolution and conflict management.* This fifth set of indicators can be used to assess (a) whether a country has affordable, clearly defined, transparent, and unbiased mechanisms for the resolution of land disputes and (b) whether these mechanisms function effectively in practice.

While the main intention is to provide a synoptic and comprehensive analysis of land governance issues that cuts across sectors, the LGAF also allows inclusion of additional sets of indicators through optional thematic modules. A module on large-scale land investments (comprising 16 additional indicators) has already been piloted, and a module on forestry has been developed. Other modules to cover topics that include financial sector management, municipal finance, natural resource management, land markets, gender and access to land, and climate change may be possible and be developed in due course.

Assessing land governance indicators through the LGAF relies on independent expert analyses that feed into meetings of expert panels to provide a consensus rating. For each country, results are summarized in a report that helps identify good practices and areas for improvement. The consistent structure of reports across countries provides a basis for comparison and identification of good practice. The methodology has been tested in five pilot countries (Peru, the Kyrgyz Republic, Tanzania, Ethiopia, and Indonesia), and the experience shows that the LGAF can be implemented over a three- to four-month period at reasonable cost. It provides a diagnostic review that identifies areas for more detailed attention, suggestions for land policy reform, and indicators—both qualitative and quantitative—that can be used to monitor improvements in land governance. Using independent local experts provides ownership and credibility to the exercise and results in an objective diagnosis that can lay the basis for better-informed policy.

Chapter 2 of this report provides a conceptual review of different land governance indicators and the way in which the LGAF addresses some of the challenges encountered. This is followed by a description of the methodology for applying the LGAF in chapter 3, a description of results from pilot countries in chapter 4, and a number of policy conclusions together with a perspective for applying the LGAF on a larger scale in chapter 5. Readers who are mainly interested in how to apply the LGAF may move directly to chapter 3 and also consult the implementation manual that is available on the web (http://econ.worldbank.org/programs/lgaf).

KEY RESULTS AND POLICY RECOMMENDATIONS FOR PILOT COUNTRIES

The country sections in the main body of this book provide a tenure typology as well as a summary of issues and recommendations based on reports that were discussed and vetted by panels at the country level. Although the reader is referred to the main text (and the online country annexes) for detail, the following discussion demonstrates that a structured review of land administration is beneficial in drawing out good-practice examples, challenges, and major lessons and policy recommendations at the country level.

Peru

Peru has a legal framework for recognizing individual or community-level land rights that entails many best-practice elements, including a very detailed process of reviewing documentary and nondocumentary evidence. Importantly, legal recognition is not limited to individual rights but extends to communal ones. However, for communal lands, lack of mapping and boundary demarcation makes it impossible to enforce property rights on the ground, leading to pervasive conflict and abuse. Enforcing the rights of Andean peasant and Amazonian native communities will require quick action to formalize these rights, to define clear territorial boundaries, and to improve these groups' representation to the outside world.

Moreover, for individually owned lands in urban areas, lack of cut-off dates for regularization, together with a tendency to periodically extend deadlines for recognition of new occupants, may create incentives for invasion and result in a cycle of invasions, resistance to eviction, and long waiting periods for infrastructure and services. Options for densification of already formalized settlements and planning of new settlements for progressive development could be more effective at helping the poor and may be worth exploring.

Legislation tightly circumscribes the cases where expropriation can be used to those that provide a public good. Congress must authorize any case of expropriation in a law that clearly identifies the future use of expropriated goods. Property values must be determined in a court proceeding, and orders lapse automatically if there is no follow-up or if the property is not used as intended within relatively tight deadlines.

Peru's constitution also enshrines legal pluralism, which recognizes, in addition to the formal system, judicial functions by relevant institutions in Andean peasant and Amazonian indigenous communities following customary law within their territories that the formal system is mandated to uphold. At the same time, the lack of a centralized information system creates an opportunity for "forum shopping" and parallel pursuit of proceedings, including manipulations to identify a judge that will best fit a party's interests.

Legal recognition, together with large-scale formalization of rights in urban and rural areas has, over the past decade, underpinned a very strong economic growth performance. Results from these initiatives could be made more sustainable by regular monitoring and efforts to reduce transaction cost, to create awareness, and to strengthen links between textual and spatial records.

The Kyrgyz Republic

The Kyrgyz Republic has experienced major land reforms during its post-Soviet transition. Although broad distribution of land to the population played an important role in the transition, the small size of individual land plots limits the income that such plots can generate. As the economy develops, land markets will assume an increasingly important role, and eliminating obstacles to their efficient functioning will be important. Pasture management will need to be improved on the basis of a recent law that decentralizes responsibility to pasture user associations and allows registration of use rights. Much progress has been made to develop a cost-effective process for first-time registration of individual rights. The new process has resulted in the registration of more than 80 percent of land parcels, including mapping and recording of the relevant private encumbrances. The registry operates in a sustainable and self-financing manner, with high levels of customer satisfaction as assessed through independent surveys.

Although much land is individually owned, the state remains the country's biggest landowner, and state land is often underused or not managed effectively.

In rural areas, 25 percent of arable agricultural land totaling some 300,000 hectares was left in state ownership to establish a temporary land reserve that was to be used to deal with land claims arising in the transition and future settlement expansion. This reserved land forms a Land Redistribution Fund (LRF) managed by local governments, which lease out the land on a short-term basis. The process, however, is often seen as not fully transparent and fails to provide either much-needed government revenue or incentives for investment and good land use. Most observers agree that the LRF is a source of corruption through underreporting of lease rates, nontransparent land management, lease agreements in the name of third parties, and fictitious enterprises qualifying for preferential treatment. Following the law and conducting allocation of LRF land through auctions, with some preference for women and disadvantaged groups, could greatly improve productivity.

With 9 million hectares or 85 percent of total agricultural land, pastures are the country's largest land use category. Nontransparent processes to award leases to such land have had very negative equity consequences. The 2009 Pasture Law replaces leases with recognition of traditional use rights, decentralizes responsibility to user associations, and allows registration at the village level. By transforming leases into use rights that allow seasonal mobility and retention of revenues from pastures by local government, this law is expected to be an important step in fostering decentralization and more sustainable use of natural resources.

Tanzania

After more than a decade of debate, Tanzania's Land Act and Village Land Act (1999) broke new ground in recognizing existing tenure regimes in Africa. In addition to some 2 percent of "general land" and 28 percent of "reserved land" (which includes forests, conservation areas, national parks, and game reserves), 70 percent of total land is classified as "village land" and is under the jurisdiction and management of registered villages. These villages can obtain a certificate of village land once they agree on boundaries with neighboring villages and, within their borders, identify land for communal and individual use and possibly a land reserve. When the LGAF was conducted in 2009, less than 800 of the more than 12,000 registered villages have received certificates, and only about 7 percent of plots on general land are registered. With some 80 percent of land in the capital city lacking formal recognition or demarcation, levels of urban informality are estimated to be among the highest in the world. Moreover, less than 20 percent of the land is registered in women's names. The relatively high level of tenure security enjoyed by occupants in settled areas, even if informal, does not extend to the marginalized and pastoralists, who often have their rights infringed upon.

High fees and unrealistic planning standards put formalization out of reach of the poor. Even high-profile efforts to increase formality had mixed success, and some two-thirds (68 percent) of urban buildings do not comply with approved plans. Transferability of land is limited by centralized, cumbersome, and costly approval processes for any transaction. Delivery of land administration services is highly centralized, with only limited authority given to local governments. Similarly, because most property tax revenue has to be transferred to central government, incentives for more effective collection by local governments are weak; only some 30 percent of potential revenue is actually collected. To address these problems, the Ministry of Lands, Housing, and Human Settlements Development needs to more effectively exercise oversight, set broad policy and guidelines, and monitor implementation. The land registry should be decentralized and provide integrated services for both village and general land rather than having two coexisting registries with plenty of scope for overlap and confusion.

Expropriation is a major problem as it is routinely used in a highly regressive manner to acquire land for subsequent transfer to private interests, either in the name of "rational town planning" or "productive rural investment." Furthermore, the expropriation process is perceived as being arbitrary, with weak, ill-defined avenues for appeal, and having unclear formulas for determining compensation that are applied in a nontransparent way. Even registered village lands can be incorporated into urban expansion through processes that involve minimal compensation, thus undermining the value of village certificates and limiting the incentives for regularization. A policy for urban land management and administration will need to be developed expeditiously to establish land use plans and to guide development of urban areas and townships in a participatory way, thereby eliminating uncertainty. Such a policy could form the basis to allow communities and the private sector to plan and survey land and to allow urban areas to cope with growth. In rural areas, land use planning, in line with existing policy, could be used to recognize and secure the rights of transhumant groups such as pastoralists, hunters, gatherers, and other vulnerable communities.

Ethiopia

Ethiopia, a federal state with considerable regional autonomy in land laws, underwent major political upheavals and dramatic shifts in the pattern of land ownership over the past four decades. In what is one of the largest, fastest, and most low-cost processes to record rural land rights globally, Ethiopia's four main regions have, over a period of three to five years, registered some 25 million rural parcels. The recording of rights has been done in a participatory, pro-poor, and gender-sensitive manner that provides many lessons for other countries. To ensure sustainability of the gains achieved, authorities must see that land records are updated to show changes over time. However, a policy of urban expansion based on unrealistic planning standards and low levels of compensation for land leads to unsustainable patterns of urban expansion and undermines rural tenure security. Also, lack of legal clarity on the nature of communal rights and ways to record or enforce them threatens to undermine equity and management of common property resources, with negative social and environmental impacts. In urban areas, there are two main systems: (a) a permit system under which landholders pay annual rents that are generally very low and (b) a newer lease system that includes a range of practices from administratively established leases for housing typically at very low payment levels, to leases allocated on the basis of auctions, which normally better reflect market prices, and negotiated lease payments. Urban records are managed by cities and municipalities using poor and complex record systems often with overlapping responsibility by various institutions.

Although land legislation is the mandate of the federal government, key policy choices have been delegated to regional states. Not all of these states have passed the corresponding laws, and detailed guidelines on how federal laws, proclamations, regulations, or directives are to be implemented and on the hierarchy of legislation are missing. A very positive aspect of the current land administration system is its high level of decentralization. However, although authority for most decisions is at the local level, guidance to inform officials at district and village levels is lacking. Defining local governance structures, roles, and mandates should be considered. A federal institution to consistently monitor implementation of key laws and regulations would be highly desirable and could help to assess how much policies are adhered to. Such monitoring could form the basis for clarification or dissemination.

Some of the restrictions on land use by peasants may be difficult to justify or implement consistently. For example, limiting inheritance to family members actually living on the land may run counter to the land policy's equity and nondiscrimination objectives and stymie development of the nonagricultural economy. Similarly, constraints on the share of land that can be leased out may limit incentives for investment and nonfarm employment; these restrictions should be reviewed. Also, informality, through squatting and informal rights, is a problem of increasing importance for land use and policy in Addis Ababa and other towns. Yet efforts to address the problem have been limited and piecemeal, often in the context of ad hoc measures that lacked clarity and uniformity. Given the size of the problem, it would be appropriate to address the issue through policy decisions at the federal level.

Indonesia

Although Indonesian law recognizes a broad spectrum of rights to rural land, tenure security is limited because the Basic Agrarian Law (BAL) applies to only the approximately 30 percent of the country's land area not classified as forestland, while on forestland—which may no longer carry any trees—tenure security is limited because occupants can obtain only temporal concessions but no formally recognized long-term rights. Also, many of the key regulations required to make the BAL operational have not been prepared or promulgated, implying that mechanisms to enforce the rights granted in principle to landowners and users (such as the recognition of group rights) are missing or, where the rights are present, they rely on processes that are lengthy and expensive. Consequently, both urban and rural areas are characterized by high levels of informality, and processes for recognizing long-term occupation are discretionary. Also, the amount of land in women's names remains limited.

While an efficient, participatory, and systematic registration process has been developed with donor assistance, its scale-up has been slower than planned. While available data vary widely, national estimates indicate that at most 38 million of the 80 million to 100 million land parcels have been registered. One reason is that less than half of registered properties are identifiable on maps. Moreover, the level of tenure security offered by registration is still limited. The cost of sporadic land registration is high, especially if costly informal fees are included. With the cost of transferring land being among the highest in the region, many efficiency-enhancing transactions will either not take place or be driven into informality.

To improve tenure security, it will be desirable to give explicit legal recognition to possession. Demarcating and registering forestland will also be critical in helping to protect public assets and provide the basis for effective management and land use planning. Allowing communities to own land, provided that they conform to minimum levels of accountability, could help ward off intrusion by outsiders, increase investment incentives, and facilitate a transition toward individual titles in cases where such titles are the most appropriate option. Recognition of a range of occupation and use patterns, including secondary ones, could significantly strengthen customary tenure and provide a basis for land use regulations (for example, requiring that certain land remain forest, linking property rights to responsibilities for sustainable management of land and forest, and defining landowners' entitlements to timber resources once concessions expire). From an institutional perspective, it will be desirable to have a single public agency in charge of public land administration (including registration) and to limit the Forest Department's responsibility to that of managing use of the land.

Decentralization greatly increased local governments' responsibilities without a commensurate increase in resources. Establishing standards for land agencies, publicizing individual offices' success in meeting those standards, holding independent audits, having independent mechanisms to handle complaints and conduct audits will all be key to improving provision of land information. A large number of alleged land-related improprieties makes it mandatory to strictly enforce penalties for land-related frauds, to honor the right of victims to reclaim loss from the offender or to be otherwise indemnified, to declare invalid registrations that have been established fraudulently, and to recognize the liability (including the possibility of dismissal) of civil servants for errors and fraud committed under their watch.

NEXT STEPS IN SCALING UP LGAF IMPLEMENTATION

Piloting of the LGAF provided valuable insights that documented its potential for implementation in a variety of contexts. Beyond the immediate benefit for the concerned countries, extending the LGAF's implementation to more countries will provide a significant contribution to the debate on land governance and shed light on land policy options based on shared experience. The use of an identical structure for a very heterogeneous set of countries was expected to allow the identification of good practices that could be transferred across countries as well as the identification of areas that, because they were problematic in a number of instances, would warrant more analytical efforts. Results of the pilots already suggest many lessons and good practices that could be transferred across countries in each of the five main areas.

A land governance monitoring and assessment partnership has been established with the International Food Policy Research Institute, the United Nations Human Settlement Program, the International Fund for Agricultural Development, the Food and Agricultural Organization of the United Nations, and the World Bank. The partnership will work toward the implementation of the LGAF in a selection of new countries and will facilitate the dissemination of lessons to feed back into the policy dialogue. This initiative will show that innovative solutions are indeed feasible and could, in turn, provide the basis for an active South-South exchange of experience.

CHAPTER ONE

Why Is a Land Governance Framework Needed?

apid changes in land use associated with economic development (or the lack thereof), climate change, urbanization, growth of demand for food and industrial materials, and the need to feed a rapidly growing population have significantly increased demand for policies that can help guide land use and define rights to services or benefits from streams associated with land. In many countries, poorly managed processes of urban expansion, concentration of poverty in slums, lack of clarity on land rights, and resulting conflicts over land have long been among the major issues that justify land administration and policy responses to strengthen tenure security and to create the preconditions for investments and economic development.

The need for appropriate management of land is also evident in a context where climate change and volatile food prices are likely to result in increased competition for fertile land in rural and peri-urban areas and in intensified internal migration to cities and their peripheries. Mitigation of climate change by reducing deforestation and carbon emissions, management of nonrenewable resources, and prevention or management of disasters are also important issues that require countries to have in place functioning land management and administration systems and clear policies regarding land.

Assessing whether these functions are effectively performed—and identifying politically and economically feasible ways to improve their performance—should thus be a key concern of governments. At the same time, in most societies—especially those at low levels of development—land is not only a key productive resource, asset, and safety net, but also a key determinant of political power (Binswanger, Deininger, and Feder 1995). While this suggests that an incremental approach to improving land governance that is attuned to the broader environment will be needed, it also highlights that putting the issue into a broader context will have important repercussions for social justice and (gender) equity that go well beyond the land sector, narrowly defined. Moreover, corruption in the land sector could force large sections of the population into informality and undermine market functioning more generally.

Governance has been be defined as "the manner in which public officials and institutions acquire and exercise the authority to shape public policy and provide public goods and services" (World Bank 2007, 67). As far as land governance is concerned, this definition includes the ways property rights to land (for groups or individuals) are defined and can be exchanged and transformed; the way in which public oversight over land use, land management, and taxation is exercised; the type of land that is state owned; the way such land is managed, acquired, and disposed of; the nature and quality of land ownership information available to the public and the ease with which it can be accessed or modified; and the way in which disputes are resolved and conflict is managed.

Increased overall emphasis on accountability and measureable outputs rather than just inputs imply that a framework for land governance that can be used both as a diagnostic tool and as a means to monitor change over time would be of great use to policy makers and practitioners. Ideally, such a framework could be applied to inform decision makers, to identify areas for land sector reform at the country level, to track progress, and to manage risks in the sector. Responding to the associated challenges requires an integrated view that brings together different types of policy that impinge on the governance of land resources. This book aims to contribute to the establishment of such a framework at the country level.

This first chapter discusses why ensuring good governance in the land sector is critical, describes the challenges that arise when trying to develop governance indicators for the land sector, draws conclusions regarding the nature and use of land governance indicators as well as the processes through which they should be gathered and disseminated, and defines the working agenda and its implication for subsequent chapters of this report.

WHY IT IS IMPORTANT TO ENSURE GOOD GOVERNANCE OF THE LAND SECTOR

An increasingly recognized and important role of the public sector is to establish and maintain institutions that define rights and make associated information on such rights freely available. The rules governing such behavior are of relevance in several respects. First, governance in the sense of the quality of institutional arrangements, adherence to the rule of law, and focus on accountability and has long been shown to affect economic outcomes at the firm level (Caprio, Laeven, and Levine 2007; Chhaochharia and Laeven 2009). Public spending in poorly governed countries has also been shown to have little, if any, positive effect (Rajkumar and Swaroop 2008). Consequently, spending resources on well-governed countries or sectors will help maximize the effectiveness of interventions on poverty and enhance economic impacts (Collier and Dollar 2002, 2004). Surprisingly, evidence shows that, in practice, aid flows may have little relationship to good governance.[1] These findings have justified and given rise to a large number of studies that provide aggregate country-level indicators of governance to be used, for example, to determine the size of foreign assistance. Although progress in this direction has so far been limited, complementing such aggregate indicators with sector-specific ones may be a precondition for more specific reforms that would in turn help improve aggregate indicators of governance (Johnson 2008).

Even in terms of standard indicators such as corruption, land has long been known to be one of the sectors most affected by bad governance—something that is not difficult to understand in light of the fact that not only is land a major asset, but also its value is likely to rise rapidly in many contexts of urbanization and economic development. The most authoritative survey of global corruption finds that, after the police and the courts, land services are the most corrupt sector, ahead of other registry and permit services, education, health, tax authorities, or public utilities (Transparency International 2009).[2]

Although individual amounts may be small, such petty corruption can add up to large sums; in India, the total amount of bribes paid annually by users of land administration services is estimated at US$700 million (Transparency International India 2005), equivalent to three-quarters of India's total public spending on science, technology, and environment. Large-scale corruption associated with acquisition and disposal of public lands is more notorious in some contexts. For example, in Kenya, land-related fraud by public officials reached systemic proportions since the 1980s and was identified as "one of the most pronounced manifestations of corruption and moral decadence in our society" (Government of Kenya 2004, 192). For private land, bad governance manifests itself in the difficulty of accessing land administration institutions to obtain land ownership information or to transfer property to another party. Together, large- and small-scale corruption will reduce the perceived integrity and, because of high transaction costs, the completeness of land registries, thereby undermining the very essence of land administration systems.

In addition to reducing opportunity for corruption and bribery, good land governance is also critical as a precondition for sustainable economic development and social justice in a number of respects (Deininger 2003).

- First, those who have only insecure or short-term land rights are unlikely to invest their full effort to make long-term improvements attached to the land. They may instead be forced to expend significant resources to defend the rights to their land, without producing benefits for the broader economy. Among the most insecure with respect to land tenure are women (especially in cases of inheritance or divorce) and other traditionally disadvantaged groups, such as migrants or herders.

- Second, if property rights are poorly defined or cannot be enforced at low cost, it will also be much harder to transfer such land between different uses. Secure land tenure facilitates the transfer of land at low cost through rentals and sales, improving the allocation of land. Without secure rights, landowners are less willing to rent out their land, which may impede their ability and willingness to engage in nonagricultural employment or rural-urban migration, thereby reducing the scope for structural change and decreasing the productivity of land use in both rural and urban areas.
- Third, setting up or expanding a business requires physical space—land. Nontransparent, corrupt, or simply inefficient systems of land administration constitute a major bottleneck that makes it more costly for small and would-be entrepreneurs to transform good ideas into economically viable enterprises.[3]
- Fourth, to the extent that easily transferable land rights may be used as collateral, their availability will reduce the cost of accessing credit for entrepreneurs, thus increasing opportunities for gainful employment and contributing to innovation and the development of financial systems.
- Finally, as a result of economic development, the increased demand for land, together with public investment in infrastructure and roads, tends to make land more valuable. In many cases, lack of well-functioning mechanisms to tax land suggests that the scope for society—in particular, local governments—to claim its legitimate share of the land rent or the increase in land values is limited. Instead, many of the gains can end up with private individuals or generate bribes, while the prospect for gains may fuel speculation and increase inequality and inefficient uses of the land. In contrast, if land institutions function properly, land taxation provides a simple yet efficient tool to increase effective decentralization and to foster local government accountability.

The need for good land governance is reinforced by three broad-based global trends. First, increased pressure on rural and urban land in response to volatile commodity prices (which provide incentives for investments in agricultural land) and population growth (often in urban and peri-urban areas) makes it more important to effectively define and protect land resources. A precondition for this process is that the benefits from opportunities for development be broadly shared. Second, climate change is likely to have particularly pernicious effects on areas traditionally considered to be hazardous or marginal. Adequate land use planning, together with land information and associated geospatial tools to manage disasters, can help governments mitigate or adapt to these effects. Finally, global programs that provide resources for environmental services, such as to reduce deforestation, are likely to affect behavior at the local level and, thus, accomplish their objectives only if local land rights are recognized to allow effective ways of channeling resources for right holders.

The effects of weak land governance will be particularly harmful for the poor in developing countries for whom land is a primary means to generate a livelihood; a key vehicle to invest, accumulate wealth, and transfer such wealth between generations; and a key part of their identity. Because land represents such a large share of the asset portfolio of the poor,[4] providing or supporting the acquisition of—secure property rights to the land they already use can increase the wealth of poor people who cannot afford the (official and unofficial) fees needed to enter the formal system. Therefore, improved land governance has great potential to directly and indirectly benefit the poor.

The above-mentioned factors have prompted a number of initiatives at national and international levels. First, an increasing number of countries implement far-reaching programs to improve land tenure, often with significant support from multilateral and bilateral institutions.[5] Second, the rising recognition of the importance of good land governance at the political level is noticeable. For example, the African Union, whose heads of state agreed in 2009 to the Framework and Guidelines for Land Policy in Africa, has called for the development of benchmarks against which to measure country performance in terms of land governance (African Union 2009).[6] Finally, in this context, the Food and Agriculture Organization of the United Nations (FAO), in partnership with other United Nations institutions, is undertaking a worldwide, broad-based process of regional consultations, which is expected to result in a set of voluntary guidelines for good governance of land and associated natural resources (FAO Land Tenure and Managment Unit 2009; Palmer, Fricska, and Wehrmann 2009). The Land Governance Assessment Framework (LGAF) presented here can provide important technical input into these initiatives and support them moving forward.

HOW GOVERNANCE IN THE LAND SECTOR IS CURRENTLY ASSESSED

Given the many facets and the cross-cutting nature of governance, a common way of assessing it has been through indicators. Indicators are measures that (a) convey information about a phenomenon or a process, (b) are based on verifiable data or information, and (c) can be interpreted within the perspective of agreed-upon policy objectives. An indicator needs to be relevant; that is, it brings meaningful information relating to the issue that is raised. An indicator needs to be accurate in the sense that it can be unambiguously derived from the underlying data that support it. Finally, it needs to be consistent, that is, a change in the indicator can be unambiguously attributed to an improvement or a deterioration of the dimensions that are assessed.

Although the literature has developed numerous governance indicators to help make the complex concept of governance operational,[7] a useful categorization distinguishes rule-based indicators from outcome-based indicators (Kaufmann and Kraay 2008). *Rule-based* indicators assess whether those institutions that are generally presumed to be associated with good governance (such as alternate dispute resolution mechanisms to address land conflicts) are in place. As long as one can identify relevant measures that are clearly linked to positive outcomes and are easily observed by outsiders, making reference to such measures facilitates assessments of governance status and progress in the land sector. However, a frequently mentioned drawback is that a large number of indicators may be needed to approximate the complexity of real-world situations. Moreover, having rules on paper often says little about the extent and quality of their implementation, although it is clearly the latter that counts and is desired.[8] *Outcome-based* indicators, by contrast, focus on either broad citizen perceptions—the extent to which (potential) users find public services to be easily accessed and responsive to their needs—or expert opinion about the de facto implementation of rules. Although outcome-based indicators provide a more differentiated picture, they are normally more costly to collect and less actionable from a policy perspective. In practice, outcome- and rule-based indicators can complement each other.[9]

Regarding the land sector, indicators based on the opinion of experts, who are presumed to be intimately familiar with the sector, have been used most frequently. Opinion is often assessed using a large number of individual dimensions for which scores are assigned and then aggregated to inform broad decisions, such as to decide on allocation of resources across competing efforts. For example, at the multilateral level, indicators to determine overall resource allocation, including the World Bank's Country Policy and Institutional Assessment and the International Fund for Agricultural Development's Performance-Based Allocation System, make implicit or explicit reference to land and property rights.[10] One important initiative is the development of the Legal and Institutional Framework Index (LIFI), developed by the United Nations Human Settlements Program (UN-Habitat) to measure security of tenure in urban contexts (see box 1.1). LIFI comprises four categories to measure security of tenure: evictions, regularization and prevention, land administration practices, and land markets.

Another initiative to assess indicators of land governance (not restricted to the urban sector) is the Blueprint for Strengthening Real Property Rights. It takes the form of a country-level analytical tool that the United States Agency for International Development prepared to support the Inter-American Alliance for Real Property Rights in benchmarking and scoring progress toward effective property rights systems in Latin America and the Caribbean (see box 1.2 for details). In light of the five principles set out in the

The Legal and Institutional Framework Index (LIFI) is a tool, designed under UN-Habitat's Strategy to Monitor Security of Tenure, to assess land tenure in urban areas using a tenure security indicator. It aggregates information regarding a country's legal, institutional, administrative, and policy environment relevant to tenure security.

The focus of the Strategy to Monitor Security of Tenure is on assessing the dynamics of tenure security as an incremental process. The tool includes an assessment of two processes: to progressively acquire tenure security and to move from informality toward formality (by strengthening institutional capacities). The process to acquire tenure security is decomposed into access to land (equality and distribution), land documentation, land transfers, and the institutional and legal framework. The process to move toward formality is decomposed into evictions, remedies, land administration practices, and land market interventions and transferability. Each process item is then broken down into dimensions that are scored depending on observed practices. For instance, the score on evictions is computed on a 25-point scale depending on stakeholders' involvement in eviction decisions at the community level (maximum 5 points); on the processes prior to eviction, that is, on consultation, justification, notification, recording, and compensation and relocation (3 points each, maximum 5 points); and on the legal aid support to the potential evictee (maximum 5 points). Scores are established based on data collected during a two-day working session with land experts of various sectors, including nongovernmental organizations, the media, lawyers, land administrators, surveyors, urban planners, and professionals from the real estate and construction sectors. A summary rating is also computed, ranging from 0 (reflecting lack of tenure security) to 1 (reflecting maximum tenure security). The assessment allows a diagnosis of the existence of laws and institutions relating to tenure rights and of inheritance and evictions, as well as a discussion on the levels of applicability of these laws.

Source: http://www.uneca.org/eca_programmes/sdd/documents/land-policy/LIFI%20 power%20point_Moreno_Habitat.ppt

blueprint, an additional set of 48 standards is also used to assess the following five functions: the ability to use rights in property as collateral (security interest), the ability to transfer rights in property (primary transactions), the publicity of rights in property (registry), the legal description of property (tenure), and the physical description of property (cadastre). These indicators are organized in a matrix. For instance, an indicator of equity under the tenure principle is whether property rights of all individuals and ethnic groups are recognized. Another recent initiative to assess land governance is from the

Box 1.2 Measuring Land Governance: The Blueprint for Strengthening Real Property Rights

The Blueprint for Strengthening Real Property Rights is a tool for benchmarking and scoring progress toward effective property rights systems. (For information on the blueprint, visit the Landnet Americas website). It is an assessment framework that relies on principles, indicators, standards, and actions.

The framework starts with a description of the country's real property rights situation that includes the systems for the cadastre, tenure, registration, primary transactions, and security of interests. It also proposes to evaluate reform readiness in terms of government vision, consensus, and political willingness.

The baseline of the template lists 16 dimensions under the headings of financial market, livelihood and social equity, fiscal revenues, and institutional progress. To assess each of the dimensions, the framework identifies data, mostly quantitative, that reflect values and financial and time costs relevant to land markets and land administration. Under the institutional progress category, for instance, one indicator is the cost of registering property transactions for first transactions and for the transfer of title to property and liens. A few indicators are qualitative and refer to the existence of institutions, such as extrajudicial mechanisms to resolve conflicting property rights.

The baseline is embedded into a broader set of 36 efficiency indicators categorized under the five main categories of comprehensiveness, efficiency, transparency, equity, and enforceability of the property rights system. This list of indicators covers a variety of topics regarding the property rights system. *Comprehensiveness* indicators assess whether many kinds of assets (real estate, movable property, and portfolio of loans) can be used to back financial transactions and whether informal property is incorporated into the registration system. A sample indicator is the percentage of real properties in the country that can be used as collateral. The *efficiency* category focuses on whether property services are performed without imposing undue cost and whether information management is modernized. Among other such indicators is the cost to regularize a parcel. *Transparency* is about whether laws and regulations are consistent and known; whether information is compatible across the registry system; and whether records may be easily obtained by those who make legitimate inquiries, particularly the right holder. For instance, an indicator focuses on whether the public has access to cadastral or registry information. *Equity* indicators explore whether the rule of law applies equally to the property of all persons without regard to gender, social stature, or ethnicity. This category includes, for example, whether regularization processes do not discriminate by gender, race, or religion. Finally, *enforceability* indicators assess whether property

(continued next page)

rights, including those by creditors, are enforceable in courts or through extrajudicial proceedings without undue delay and whether there are disincentives, in fact or in law, for undue delay in relation to administrative and judicial processes. For instance, this category includes an indicator on whether defense or protection of property rights is obtained through fast, low-cost processes.

Source: http://www.landnetamericas.org/docs/allianceBlueprint.pdf

French Development Agency and the French Ministry for the Economy, Industry and Employment, and includes a set of land governance variables in the governance database that they maintain and that covers 123 countries.[11]

An advantage of this approach is that such indicators can be collected at low cost and, with appropriate explanations, can be actionable. At the same time, the relevance of ratings depends on the qualifications of the experts engaged in the assessment of the indices; any doubts raised concerning the qualifications or personal biases of the relevant experts affect the credibility of the overall assessment. The ability to compare within the same country over time may also be limited, especially if the experts involved change over time.

Representative surveys of households, users, or intermediaries (such as lawyers) in accessing public services do not suffer from these drawbacks and thus may provide a better assessment of outcomes that can be compared over time. However, the size of samples required to obtain estimates that capture variations within a country can be quite large, potentially making such efforts quite costly. To reduce costs, the World Bank's Doing Business indicators (World Bank 2009) are undertaken by experts who are asked to provide estimates for a hypothetical case that is frequently encountered by entrepreneurs and is highly actionable in one or two dimensions. The experts are asked to identify the required actions and associated cost for this hypothetical situation.

Regarding property, the focus is on registration of a plot of a given size, free of conflict and other encumbrances, and for industrial use on the periphery of the country's capital. Though the Doing Business indicators have been effective in drawing attention to the topic and prompting policy reform, the meaning of registration—and, thus, the associated requirements—differs across legal systems, and the failure to adjust for those differences can reduce the relevance and usefulness of such indicators (Arrunada 2007).[12] This lack of adjustment may fail to appropriately capture the country-specific nature and nuances of land administration systems (Arrunada 2007) or give more specific policy recommendations. The Doing Business indicators, which have a strong empirical basis, have been highly effective for efforts that focus on policy reform in one or two areas, such as the reduction of transaction costs and transfer fees. At the same time, the relevance of these indicators may be limited in some places, especially in Africa, where often 90 percent and more of landholders are not registered.

Besides the collection of information through experts or representative household surveys, local land observatories offer yet another approach for monitoring land governance. They are often run by civil society groups and are linked to advocacy or educational efforts, aiming to actively improve governance in the land sector.[13] Their effectiveness over the longer term, however, has been limited by the lack of a common and agreed-upon framework; by the difficulty of accessing information on the performance of land administration institutions; and, sometimes, by the lack of institutional legitimacy and recognition by the other institutions in the land sector. This implies that a framework should draw significantly on local expertise in a structured way so as to be comparable and to draw attention to examples of good practices in other contexts that can be referenced and drawn upon in similar areas.

THE CHALLENGES OF ADDRESSING LAND GOVERNANCE

Why, then, has there not been more progress in land governance? Three reasons relate to (a) the technical complexity of land management and administration and the need to make policy trade-offs; (b) the political sensitivity and, in many cases, institutional fragmentation of the land sector; and (c) the country-specific and sometimes local nature of land tenure arrangements that makes simple institutional transplants impossible. Land administration is technically complex and cuts across many disciplines, such as law; information technology; geodesy; geomatics and surveying; economics; urban planning; anthropology; and environmental, social, and political sciences. Some of these fields are rapidly advancing, making it important not to remain with outdated solutions but rather to design systems in a way that anticipates future improvements. A key challenge is also to make trade-offs that help improve overall system performance rather than focus on over-engineered approaches that may be appropriate from a disciplinary perspective but weigh down the system and eventually make it unsustainable.[14] While these trade-offs are ultimately a policy decision, a framework for the land sector can help to identify key areas of concern and guide support for developing an integrated strategy.

Because control of land is a key determinant of economic and often political power, the land sector is intensely political. This explains the fact that in many countries, the sector is characterized by a high level of institutional fragmentation, in which, contrary to sectors such as education or health, the responsibility for formulation and implementation of land policy is dispersed among ministries and institutions in different sectors (for example, lands, justice, finance, agriculture, forestry, environment, urban affairs and housing, and mining and energy). The division of responsibility between central and local government institutions adds further complexity that often results in uncoordinated actions and high transaction costs. To deal with this complexity, one must take a holistic view and focus on objectively measurable information based on technical issues rather than base assessments on value judgments and subjective perceptions that could be interpreted as politically motivated.

Land rights and tenure arrangements have evolved over long periods in response to ecological conditions and resource endowments and often reflect societies' values and norms. In many countries, external factors such as colonization have significantly affected land administration arrangements and institutions. Attempts to assess land institutions that fail to draw on local knowledge and instead try to impose one-size-fits-all solutions are unlikely to be effective because the solutions may not be appropriate to the specific characteristics of a given location. Initiatives undertaken without local knowledge or out of sequence (for example, surveying or titling without a policy framework to secure rights and ensure an accessible and transparent process) have often had undesirable impacts.

A number of initiatives have aimed to combine existing governance indicators in innovative ways to summarize those that are already of relevance to local governance (for example, the International Property Rights Index under the patronage of Hernando de Soto).[15] But coming up with an effective tool to assess land sector governance that could serve as a basis for diagnosis and policy dialogue is likely to require a more specific and much more detailed approach. Ideally, a tool to help with this would be based on a diagnostic review that generates data in a replicable and cost-effective way, characterized by four criteria: (a) sufficient standardization to allow qualitative comparison across countries and, more important, identification of good practices that could be transferred between countries; (b) use of quantitative information as much as possible to provide ways to eliminate subjectivity, to verify information, and to compare over time and (ideally) across locations within a country; (c) comprehensive coverage of relevant issues and a link to actionable policy prescriptions; and (d) applicability at sufficiently low cost to generate debate and consensus among stakeholders to allow follow-up measurement and to contribute to substantive harmonization and coordination.

APPROACH AND STRUCTURE OF THE REPORT

To move towards this goal, a first step was to define the coverage of land governance by identifying substantive focus areas, based on the key functions that the public sector needs to perform in the land sector. Five areas were defined in this way (see chapter 2). The second step was to develop a methodology to obtain information and arrive at an assessment that is robust and legitimate and draws on local expertise. Chapter 3 describes how the LGAF addresses this through methodological gathering of prior information, involvement of local experts, and synthesis of these elements made by an expert country coordinator. Finally, the third step was the application of the framework on a pilot basis in five countries that are characterized by very diverse contexts and land policies—Ethiopia, Indonesia, the Kyrgyz Republic, Peru, and Tanzania. The main results from these pilots are presented in chapter 4. Because the intention was not only to derive substantive lessons for the study countries, but also to learn lessons that would allow refinement of the LGAF approach and its operational methodology, chapter 5 highlights substantive and methodological insights, drawing out implications for possible future rollout of the LGAF.

NOTES

1. Busse and Groning (2009) and Knack (2009) found that, in practice, aid flows have no relationship to good governance, suggesting that there is still considerable scope for improvement. A commitment to focusing assistance on countries or sectors with good governance is a key trend that underlies the movement toward sector-wide support and greater responsibility of governments (Hout 2007).
2. In land services, 15 percent of users have had to pay a bribe, putting it after police (24 percent) and the judiciary (16 percent) but ahead of other registry and permit services (13 percent), education and health (both 9 percent), and tax revenues or utilities (both 7 percent).
3. World Bank investment climate surveys indicate that access to land is the main obstacle to conducting and expanding business in 57 percent of the enterprises interviewed in Ethiopia, in 35 percent in Bangladesh, and in about 25 percent each in Tanzania and Kenya.
4. Most household surveys indicate that land constitutes between one-half and two-thirds of the asset endowment by the poorest households.
5. The World Bank alone supervises a portfolio of dedicated land projects totaling US$1.5 billion. Other donors provide large amounts of support as well.
6. The African heads of state endorsed at their July 2009 summit a framework and guidelines for land policy, with an explicit mandate to effectively monitor and regularly report on progress with implementation. Thus, technical input will be needed to help translate these principles into practice, to make the transition from problem identification to actionable policy and institutional reforms, and to generate resources for implementing them. The European Union also adopted a set of land policy guidelines.
7. For lists of indicators, see Langbein and Knack (2010).
8. For example, in all countries covered by the World Bank's 2006 Worldwide Governance Indicators (http://info.worldbank.org/governance/wgi/index.asp), taking a bribe is officially considered illegal. All but three (Brazil, Lebanon, and Liberia) had anticorruption commissions (Kaufmann and Kraay 2008).
9. Other useful categories of indicators are based on their function. *Descriptive indicators* give information on the present situation with regard to a particular issue (for example, surface of the land in the custody of the state). *Performance indicators* measure the distance between the current situation and a desired situation (for

example, increase of land documentation within a given period). *Efficiency indicators* give information on the way a process is implemented or a service is delivered (such as the unit cost of registering property or use rights).

10. The World Bank's Country Policy and Institutional Assessment, which can be used to determine the allocation of International Development Association resources, includes property rights as one of 16 areas: macroeconomic management; fiscal policy; debt policy; trade; financial sector; business regulatory environment; gender equality; equity of public resource use; building human resources; social protection and labor; policies and institutions for environmental sustainability; property rights and rule-based governance; quality of budgetary and financial management; efficiency of revenue mobilization; quality of public administration; and transparency, accountability, and corruption in the public sector. (For details, see International Development Association, "How IDA Resources Are Allocated," http://go.worldbank.org/F5531ZQHT0.) The International Fund for Agricultural Development's performance-based allocation system is targeted more specifically to rural areas and includes an explicit indicator for access to land under its five broad headings: strengthening the capacity of the rural poor and their organizations, improving equitable access to productive natural resources and technology, increasing access to financial services and markets, gender issues, and public resource management and accountability (IFAD 2009). Millennium Challenge Corporation, a U.S. foreign aid agency, explicitly refers to land when determining a country's eligibility to sign a compact with the adoption of the "doing business" indicators for the cost and time required to register a property and the IFAD indicator for access to land.

11. See the Institutional Profiles Database 2009, http://www.cepii.fr/anglaisgraph/bdd/institutions.htm.

12. Global indicators on the cost and time required to register land, collected since 2004 by the International Finance Corporation for the main city in any given country on the basis of expert opinion, have received considerable attention by policy makers and development partners. Several extensions are currently under way.

13. An example is the Madagascar land observatory created in 2007, which is responsible for following up with implementation of reforms, impact evaluation, and discussion of policy orientation. The land observatory conveys its observations and advice to the government and other actors in the land sector as well as externally through a periodic publication. The Madagascar observatory has been very active in providing advice on the implementation of the land reform and addresses issues as diverse as the setting of land administration fees, the introduction of local taxation, or the building of decentralized land administration capacity.

14. Classic examples are laws that were written without considering the technical feasibility or affordability of implementation; parcel survey standards that are out of line with the capacity and time available for implementation; land use or planning regulations that push most existing land users into informality with the stroke of a pen; large-scale efforts at surveying that lack an appropriate policy framework; a clear, transparent, and well-publicized process for adjudicating rights; or a functioning system of registration to ensure that up-to-date information can be maintained.

15. The International Property Rights Index combines, under its physical property rights category, an indicator of protection of physical property rights and an indicator of access to loans from the World Economic Forum's Global Competitiveness Index, as well as an indicator of property registration from the World Bank's Doing Business indicators. See Strokova (2009) for more details.

REFERENCES

African Union. 2009. "Land Policy in Africa: A Framework to Strengthen Land Rights, Enhance Productivity and Secure Livelihoods." African Development Bank, the African Union, and Economic Commission for Africa, Addis Ababa.

Arrunada, B. 2007. "Pitfalls to Avoid When Measuring Institutions: Is Doing Business Damaging Business?" *Journal of Comparative Economics* 35 (4): 729–47.

Binswanger, H. P., K. Deininger, and G. Feder. 1995. "Power, Distortions, Revolt, and Reform in Agricultural Land Relations." In *Handbook of Development Economics*, vol. 3B, ed. J. Behrman and T. N. Srinivasan, 2659–772. Amsterdam: Elsevier Science.

Busse, M., and S. Groning. 2009. "Does Foreign Aid Improve Governance?" *Economic Letters* 104 (2): 76–78.

Caprio, G., L. Laeven, and R. Levine. 2007. "Governance and Bank Valuation." *Journal of Financial Intermediation* 16 (4): 584–617.

Chhaochharia, V., and L. Laeven. 2009. "Corporate Governance Norms Practices." *Journal of Financial Intermediation* 18 (3): 405–31.

Collier, P., and D. Dollar. 2002. "Aid Allocation and Poverty Reduction." *European Economic Review* 46 (8): 1475–1500.

———. 2004. "Development Effectiveness: What Have We Learnt?" *Economic Journal* 114 (496): F244–F271.

Deininger, K. 2003. *Land Policies for Growth and Poverty Reduction: A World Bank Policy Research Report*. New York: Oxford University Press; Washington, DC: World Bank.

FAO (Food and Agriculture Organization of the United Nations) Land Tenure and Managment Unit. 2009. "Towards Voluntary Guidelines on Responsible Governance of Tenure of Land and Other Natural Resources." Land Tenure Working Paper 10, FAO, Rome.

Government of Kenya. 2004. *Report of the Commission of Inquiry into the Illegal/Irregular Allocation of Public Land*. Nairobi: Government Printer.

Hout, W. 2007. *The Politics of Aid Selectivity: Good Governance Criteria in World Bank, US, and Dutch Development Assistance*. London and New York: Routledge.

IFAD (International Fund for Agricultural Development). 2009. "Progress Report on Implementation of the Performance Based Allocation System." IFAD, Rome.

Johnson, S. 2008. "Comment—Governance Indicators: Where Are We, Where Should We Be Going?" *World Bank Research Observer* 23 (1): 31–34.

Kaufmann, D., and A. Kraay. 2008. "Governance Indicators: Where Are We, Where Should We Be Going?" *World Bank Research Observer* 23 (1): 1–30.

Knack, S. 2009. "Sovereign Rents and Quality of Tax Policy and Administration." *Journal of Comparative Economics*, 37 (3): 359–71.

Langbein, L., and S. Knack. 2010. "The Worldwide Governance Indicators: Six, One, or None?" *Journal of Development Studies* 46 (2): 350–70.

Palmer, D., S. Fricska, and B. Wehrmann. 2009. "Towards Improved Land Governance." Land Tenure Working Paper 11, FAO and United Nations Human Settlements Programme, Rome.

Rajkumar, A. S., and V. Swaroop. 2008. "Public Spending and Outcomes: Does Governance Matter?" *Journal of Development Economics* 86 (1): 96–111.

Strokova, V. 2009. "International Property Rights Index 2010 Report." Property Rights Alliance, Washington, DC.

Transparency International. 2009. "Global Corruption Barometer 2009." Transparency International, Berlin.

Transparency International India. 2005. "India Corruption Study 2005." Transparency International, New Delhi.

World Bank. 2007. *Strengthening World Bank Group Engagement on Governance and Anticorruption.* Washington, DC: Joint Ministerial Committee of the Boards of Governors of the World Bank and the Fund on the Transfer of Real Resources to Developing Countries.

———. 2009. *Doing Business in 2010: Reforming through Difficult Times.* Washington, DC: World Bank, International Finance Corporation, and Oxford University Press.

CHAPTER TWO

Areas Covered by the Land Governance Assessment Framework

Before trying to assess or measure land governance, one must clearly understand the role to be fulfilled by public institutions in the land sector. This role is essentially threefold. First, countries need a legal and institutional framework that clearly defines the rules for allocation of property rights and, by allowing cost-effective enforcement, encourages and facilitates land-related investment. Second, reliable and complete information on land and property rights needs to be freely available to interested parties. Access to land information would then allow for low-cost verification of land-ownership status, which in turn would form the basis for low-cost land transfers to more productive use or users and may facilitate the use of property as collateral in financial markets. Finally, regulations are needed to avoid negative externalities that may arise from uncoordinated action by private parties. Weak governance of the land sector and a failure to perform these functions effectively will negatively affect development by reducing investment levels, property transfers, financial sector activity, and the scope for meaningful decentralization. At the same time, weak governance will contribute to elevated levels of tenure insecurity and conflict and possibly degradation of natural resources. Because the poor lack other assets, access to land is more important to them, and consequently, bad land governance will have undesirable distributional consequences and disproportionately hurt the poor.

The above functions led to the identification of five key areas of good land governance:

- A legal, institutional, and policy framework that recognizes existing rights, enforces them at low cost, and allows users to exercise them in line with their aspirations and in a way that benefits society as a whole.
- Arrangements for land use planning and taxation that avoid negative externalities and support effective decentralization.
- Clear identification of state land and its management in a way that cost-effectively provides public goods; use of expropriation only as a last resort and only for direct public purposes with quick payment of fair compensation and effective mechanisms for appeal; and mechanisms for divestiture of state lands that are transparent and maximize public revenue.
- Public provision of land information in a way that is broadly accessible, comprehensive, reliable, current, and cost-effective in the long run.
- Accessible mechanisms to authoritatively resolve disputes and manage conflict, with clearly defined mandates and low cost of operation.

Justifications for each of these areas and the 21 Land Governance Indicators (LGIs) that underpin the assessment of land governance for these areas as well as ways to make them operational are discussed below.

LEGAL AND INSTITUTIONAL FRAMEWORK

A good legal and institutional framework implies that long-standing rights by existing land users are recognized (not necessarily only for those holding a formal right, with a clear demonstration of the recognition of rights evident in the eligibility for compensation in case of expropriation). Also, the state has institutions and policies in place that allow right holders to easily enforce their rights and exercise them in line with their values and aspirations and in ways that benefit society as a whole.

Recognition of Rights (LGI 1)

Because failure to recognize existing rights will create tenure insecurity, curb investments in land, increase the potential for conflict, and divert resources that can be more productively deployed elsewhere to the defense of property claims, the legal recognition of existing land rights is a key element of good land governance. Failure to clearly identify or define land rights, including individual, secondary, usufruct, customary, or other types of group rights, can reduce the ease of making transactions, thereby blocking the movement of land to more efficient uses and possibly its use as collateral. In traditional systems, rights held by women, children, and vulnerable groups such as migrants or herders are often insufficiently protected, come under threat as land values increase, or are in danger of being appropriated by the better-off or the well informed. Thus, in a dynamic environment, special safeguards are needed to ensure that such rights are protected. In many developing countries' practice, within a given country or jurisdiction, different rights are likely to coexist (legal pluralism) and evolve over time. This suggests a need for flexibility in the types of rights that can be recognized and in the ways rights can be upgraded. At the same time, it is important that rights be administered transparently and cost-effectively and in a way that has local legitimacy. In particular, as long as the choice in favor of communal ownership arrangements is made by users on the basis of careful and informed consideration of the advantages and disadvantages of different arrangements, such choices should be respected and protected. To the contrary, if rights are not formally recognized but accountable structures exist within communities, and if arrangements can be revisited as circumstances change, the identification and registration of community boundaries can be a very cost-effective way to cover large areas within limited time and resource requirements.

Enforcement of Rights (LGI 2)

To allow the effective protection against competing claims, legal recognition needs to be backed by the ability of right holders to unambiguously identify land boundaries and call upon the powers of the state to defend their rights if they are challenged. If an increased frequency of transfers makes it more likely for competing claims to arise (a phenomenon generally observed as land becomes more valuable), then registration to put existing rights, as well as transfers of these rights, on public record is normally worth the cost, especially if low-cost mechanisms are employed to do so. To the extent that registration implies formality, it can be complemented by a focus on the recording of tenure situations among the continuum of rights, which can involve simple and cost-effective means already practiced by local populations. If rights are assigned to groups, then regulations will be needed to address how such groups can organize themselves, decide on internal rules, interact with outsiders, and call on external agencies to enforce rules.

Mechanisms for Recognition of Rights (LGI 3)

Although putting land rights on record will not miraculously transform an economy through a sudden emergence of credit markets, mechanisms to formalize rights in a way that respects existing arrangements are often justified if land values and the frequency of transactions increase. However, if existing land rights are unclear or weak, using a sporadic or an on-demand approach for the first-time registration of rights can carry a significant risk of land being concentrated in the hands of well-connected and powerful elites. Systematic registration efforts can reduce these dangers by including ways (a) to inform all potential claimants about the processes and criteria used to decide between competing rights, (b) to force claimants to come forward, and (c) to adjudicate rights at one point in time. Normally, systematic registration also achieves significantly lower unit cost than does sporadic registration, especially in sparsely populated areas.[1] Even where a systematic process of registration has been adopted, ways to upgrade tenure on a demand-driven basis will be needed, and mechanisms to do so should be affordable, transparent, and consistent with existing tenure practices.[2]

Restrictions on Rights (LGI 4)

Though user groups or society at large can impose limits on the types of rights or the ways in which these rights can be exercised by individual right holders, such limits should be based on a careful assessment of the cost and benefit of different options, should aim to achieve desired impacts (environmental, health, security, or other) at low cost, and should not disproportionately affect certain groups of right holders. Restrictions that are beyond the reach of large portions of right holders usually result in increased informality and reduced respect for the law. Although such restrictions can give rise to high costs of evasion and discretionary enforcement, which are not consistent with principles of good land governance, their removal may be opposed by vested interests.

Clarity of Institutional Mandates (LGI 5)

Public sector functions related to land are normally performed by different institutions, and as long as capacity is available, routine administrative tasks should be decentralized. Unclear or overlapping mandates and functions increase transaction costs and can create opportunities for discretion that undermine good governance and can push users into informality. They can also create parallel structures that threaten the integrity and reliability of the documents and information provided by land sector institutions, rendering policy implementation difficult.

Equity and Nondiscrimination in the Decision-Making Process (LGI 6)

The legitimacy of land sector institutions and the actions they perform depends on the extent to which the policy framework guiding institutional activities is backed by social consensus rather than by the perception of them being captured by special interest groups. Land policy is thus most appropriately developed in a participatory and transparent process that clearly articulates policy goals, identifies different institutional responsibilities, and includes an assessment of the resources needed for quick and effective implementation. It is important to define ways to measure progress toward achieving land policy goals and to clearly assign the responsibility for monitoring and publicizing progress toward meeting those goals—in ways that can be understood by those affected and that can feed into the policy dialogue. Responsibilities for monitoring should be assigned to ministries on the basis of information available to them.

LAND USE PLANNING, MANAGEMENT, AND TAXATION

The identification and, in many cases, the recording of land rights is essential to provide sound land management incentives. At the same time, rights come with responsibilities and obligations, and there is a clear social interest in having land used in a way that cost-effectively provides public goods and avoids negative externalities. Moreover, especially at low levels of development when other revenue sources are limited, land taxation can help support decentralization and encourage effective land use.

Transparency of Land Use Restrictions (LGI 7)

Although land use planning is justified to allow effective provision of public goods in a way consistent with available resources, good governance requires that a number of functions be met. First, land use plans and regulations should be able to cope with future land demands, avoid unrealistic standards that would force large parts of the population into informality, and be implemented effectively.[3] Their design should consider the affordability of compliance, the resources needed for effective enforcement, and the availability of mechanisms to bring reality in line with existing regulations. Planning or building standards that are beyond the reach of the majority of the population, even if sound from an engineering perspective, may undermine good land governance without leading to better land use. At the same time, participatory land use planning can, in many situations, provide an opportunity to record secondary rights (such as those by herders) that extend across large areas in a way that is more cost-effective than individual registration.

Efficiency in the Land Use Planning Process (LGI 8)

Economic development will innovatively entail changes in the way land is used or managed. However, such changes should provide benefits to society at large, rather than to specific groups; be transparent; and be implemented in a way that holds decision makers accountable. Rezoning, especially at the peri-urban fringe, can lead to large changes in land values. Having insider information on planned regulations or construction of infrastructure ahead of their actual implementation can allow those "in the know" to acquire land in anticipation and to capture potentially huge rents. To prevent speculative land acquisition, and the associated dangers of corruption, changes in zoning regulations and major infrastructure construction should be decided transparently with broad participation, be well advertised before their actual imposition, and be combined with measures (such as capital gains taxes or betterment levies) that would allow the public to capture a significant part of the generated surplus. Similarly, considerations of equity and fairness dictate that those who acquired land rights in good faith should be compensated for damages imposed by land use restrictions. Good governance also requires that land use planning avoids conflicts of interest arising from the fact that the same government institution or individual imposes land use plans and regulations, hears appeals, and possibly even acts as the ultimate land owner.

Speed and Predictability of Applications for Restricted Land Uses (LGI 9)

Although there is a social interest in having land use adhere to certain minimum standards to avoid negative externalities, routine requests for building and development permits should be handled promptly and predictably (and can in fact be contracted out). Slow and opaque processes can lead to inefficient resource allocations that hinder investment and economic development by imposing uncertainty and unnecessary costs on potential developers.

Transparency in Land Valuation and Tax Collection Efficiency (LGIs 10 and 11)

The ability to raise revenue and to decide on desired levels of service provision at the local level is a key feature of effective decentralization. Taxes on land or property are among the best sources of self-sustaining local revenues. However, this instrument is typically not used to its full potential and can encourage speculation through the idle holding of land in anticipation of large capital gains and rent seeking. Land taxation will be made more attractive if (a) local governments are allowed to retain a large part of the property tax revenue they collect, (b) they are provided with the technical means (for example, cadastres) to do so, and (c) clear principles are established for valuation and regular updating of valuation rolls to avoid arbitrariness. Though none of these measures pose technical challenges, they may be resisted by those who would be required to pay significant amounts of taxes.

MANAGEMENT OF PUBLIC LAND

Public land ownership is justified if public goods (such as infrastructure or parks) are provided or if land is used by public bodies (such as schools, hospitals, defense, or state enterprises). At the same time, the way in which state land (broadly defined as land in the custody of the state) is managed, acquired, and divested often poses serious governance challenges. To minimize such risks, it is important that (a) state land with economic value be clearly identified on the ground, (b) expropriation be implemented promptly and transparently with effective appeals mechanisms and used only as a last resort to provide public goods if direct negotiation is not feasible, and (c) public land that does not provide public goods be divested using transparent mechanisms and methods that maximize public revenue.

Identification and Clear Management of Public Land (LGI 12)

Effective management of public land is virtually impossible if there is no inventory of such land or if its boundaries are ambiguously defined. Having an inventory of economically valuable public land that includes identification of the boundaries of such land is an essential prerequisite for the proper management of this important public asset. The absence of such an inventory creates opportunities for well-connected individuals to capture state assets through informal occupation and squatting, often with negative environmental impacts. Also, information on revenues on public lands and the costs incurred to manage public lands should be open for public scrutiny, and the relevant institutions should be adequately staffed and resourced.

Justification, Time Efficiency, Transparency, and Fairness of Expropriation Procedures (LGIs 13 and 14)

Inappropriate use of the state's powers of expropriation can pose serious challenges to good governance. To avoid such problems, the state's acquisition of land will need to be carefully regulated and monitored.[4] Although expropriation can be justified to prevent moral hazard and holdout problems by private owners, its wide implementation raises the risk of public officials using their powers in ways that promote private rather than public interests and that can encourage rent seeking and political meddling.[5] Even in cases where expropriations may be justified, regulations for implementing them can suffer from deficiencies (for example, lack of consultation or mechanisms for appeal). Where needed and justified, expropriation procedures should thus be clear and transparent, with fair compensation in kind or cash at market values made available expeditiously. The key principle is that land transfer rights should be based on users' voluntary and informed agreement and should provide the right holder with fair compensation. Independent valuation of land assets should thus be the norm, where possible, when market systems for valuation have been established. Those whose land rights are affected will need access to mechanisms for appeal that can provide authoritative rulings quickly and in an independent and objective way. Land rights under consideration should extend beyond landowners to tenants and dependents (that is, spouses and children) and should also include those affected by rezoning and land use changes (that is, farmers affected by expansion of urban boundaries). Maintaining a given standard of living for those affected should be a key compensation objective.

Transparency of Public Land Allocation (LGI 15)

In cases in which the state owns more land than it should or can effectively manage—for example, because of historical reasons such as major land holdings by the military in capital cities—transfer or lease of such land can be an important way to increase the public supply of land or to use the generated revenue to provide public goods. In many contexts, divestiture of government land is one of the most egregious forms of weak governance, outright corruption (for example, bribery of government officials to obtain public land at a fraction of market value), and squandering of public wealth. Avoiding such practices will require developing divestiture processes that are clear, transparent, and competitive; publicizing any payments to be received and the extent to which they are collected; and subjecting the relevant institutions to regular and independent audits.

PUBLIC PROVISION OF LAND INFORMATION

Cost-effective provision of land information through registries has traditionally been at the heart of titling and registration programs. Although such programs often have contributed to positive outcomes, they also have often failed to reach their objectives in terms of outreach, equity, and sustainability. Those instances point to a need to ensure that registries provide broad, cost-effective access to comprehensive, reliable, up-to-date information on land ownership and relevant encumbrances. A regular assessment of the extent to which programs provide this information can be an important element to help improve land governance.

Completeness and Reliability (LGIs 16 and 17)

Because potential investors cannot be sure whether any gaps in the data available from the land registry could be relevant to their interests, they will derive few benefits from registries that do not provide complete, geographically extensive, and reliable information. If unsure, they will need to check land ownership information on a case-by-case basis. The most extreme form of ensuring reliability of land registries is for the state to indemnify individuals for losses suffered from deficient information in the registry, an institutional characteristic that is often (but not always) associated with systems of title registration. However, what matters is not the legal guarantee but the quality of the underlying information and, provided good-quality information is available, the ability of the state to actually honor any promise of indemnification. The fact that some deeds systems include a promise of indemnification for errors suggests that the type of system is not the only variable to be considered.[6] It is thus critical that registry information be accessible to interested parties and be complete, up-to-date, timely, and sufficient to make relevant inferences on ownership or on any economically relevant encumbrances.

Cost-Effectiveness, Accessibility, and Sustainability (LGIs 18 and 19)

Even if documenting land rights and their boundaries has clear benefits, the sustainability of land registries[7] and their ability to reach out to those with limited resources will depend critically on this being done in a low-cost manner. Failure to choose designs with a low cost of operation has often led to the establishment of registries that either failed to achieve full coverage or became outdated as soon as subsidies to their operation stopped. The reason is that users who are unwilling to pay large amounts of money to register subsequent transactions fail to register and revert back to informality.[8] Ensuring that operations are efficient, that fees and taxes are collected transparently, and that their magnitude and incidence is in line with equity objectives is a precondition for having a registry that serves the needs of all sectors of society and that therefore remains current and authoritative. Rather than trying to squeeze the cost of operation to unrealistically low levels—a measure that could create governance challenges of its own—cost should be kept low through the adoption of appropriate technology, especially regarding the required precision of ground surveys.[9] The fact that in some countries such efforts were opposed by a few surveyors who, by controlling entry, maintained a de facto monopoly on the market, points to the importance of governance and political economy considerations that underlie these rather technical choices.

DISPUTE RESOLUTION AND CONFLICT MANAGEMENT

Given the secular forces affecting land values, the magnitude of the resources and the vested interests at stake, and the rapid pace of social and economic change experienced by many developing countries, it may be naive to assume that conflicts over land can be avoided. What is more important from the point of view of land governance as well as social justice is to ensure that potential sources of conflict are handled in a consistent fashion rather than on an ad hoc basis and that institutions to resolve disputes and manage conflict are accessible, have clearly defined mandates, and work effectively.

Clear Assignment of Responsibility (LGI 20)

To prevent either large-scale opportunistic behavior and erosion of authority or a high level of persistent conflict that might escalate with socially disruptive consequences, conflict resolution institutions should be legitimate, accessible to most of the population, and legally authorized to resolve conflicts. Failure on any of these counts can lead to "forum shopping," whereby those with better knowledge or connections choose channels of dispute resolution that are most likely to yield an outcome that is favorable to them, or even simultaneously pursue conflict resolution in multiple forums. In many cases, efforts to avoid forum shopping will require recognizing the verdicts reached by local bodies for conflict resolution (subject to their not violating basic norms of equity and transparency) to ensure that those making decisions have basic legal knowledge and to ensure that decisions can be appealed relatively quickly.

Low Level of Pending Conflicts (LGI 21)

Continuing dispute that cannot be resolved authoritatively can impose huge costs, not only on individuals, but also on society as a whole, because it will sterilize land from investment and development. Therefore, although the wide variety of potential conflicts and the differences in legal and social norms make it difficult to assess the effectiveness of legal institutions,[10] minimum criteria, such as having a low and decreasing share of land users or plots affected by pending conflicts, can be defined.

NOTES

1. Sporadic approaches can be flexible, but minimum procedural safeguards and standards for reliability and quality of information are critical.
2. This approach to registration requires giving particular attention to documentary and nondocumentary forms of evidence to obtain recognition of claims to property. Tax receipts are often the only documentary evidence available, and cost-effective ways of using them are an important area to be explored.
3. Because unaffordable regulations (for land use or survey accuracy) can be a source of large rents, their removal may be opposed by vested interests.
4. Regulatory takings (that is, imposition of broad restrictions on land use such as those for environmental purposes) are discussed under LGI 4.
5. If actions by the public sector are slow and unpredictable or parties risk being dragged into politics, private operators may be better off acquiring land through a negotiated process. An example that has received great publicity is the attempt to acquire land on which to build a car factory in West Bengal. As expropriation proceedings became highly politicized, the project failed to materialize. In Peru, there are tight limits on expropriation, and entrepreneurs prefer to negotiate directly with land users.
6. With modern technology, deeds systems can also provide reliable information that allows checking for possible preexisting claims and includes protection against malfeasance.
7. Though data are limited on reversion to informality after systematic titling campaigns, available studies suggest that the magnitudes involved can be large (Barnes and Griffith-Charles 2007). More rigorous quantitative assessment of this issue would be highly desirable.
8. Having realistic fee schedules and paying employees competitive wages are important to preventing intermediaries and registry officials from relying on bribes to provide quick or high-quality services, further increasing the cost to

users. The culture of corruption is one of the reasons why land administration ranks so high in any independent assessments of governance.

9. Systematic documentation on the trade-offs involved would be highly desirable.

10. This difficulty would be a subject of more detailed analysis under justice reform programs.

REFERENCE

Barnes, G., and C. Griffith-Charles. 2007. "Assessing the Formal Land Market and Deformalization of Property in St. Lucia." *Land Use Policy* 24 (2): 494–501.

Government of Kenya. 2004. *Report of the Commission of Inquiry into the Illegal/Irregular Allocation of Public Land*. Nairobi: Government Printer.

CHAPTER THREE

The Methodology for Applying the Land Governance Assessment Framework

A methodology and process are needed to make sector-specific indicators of land governance policy relevant and to use them as a diagnostic tool to assess a country's situation and, according to the identified shortcomings, to define a set of policy recommendations or areas for future research. This chapter describes the overall framework used to guide such an assessment, the various ways to assemble background information, and the process adopted to create a consensus rating system that is sufficiently robust to be presented to policy makers.

THE ASSESSMENT FRAMEWORK

To summarize information in a structured way that can be understood by policy makers and allows quick identification of good practice country examples, the Land Governance Assessment Framework (LGAF) builds on the methodology used by the Public Expenditure and Financial Accountability (PEFA) assessment tool.[1] We follow PEFA by using the five thematic areas that we identified as a basis for the 21 Land Governance Indicators (LGIs) described in chapter 2. Each indicator relates to a basic principle of land governance and is then further broken down into two to six dimensions for which objective empirical information can be obtained, at least in principle. The result is the LGAF, with a total of 80 dimensions, which was developed on the basis of experience in various countries and can be used for assessing any country using objective information (Table 3.1 lists the dimensions grouped by indicator and thematic areas). Each dimension is scored by selecting an appropriate answer among a list of precoded statements that have been drafted on the basis of extensive interaction with land professionals and refined through the pilot country case studies. The general framework to structure information in a comparable way is adopted from PEFA, with four key differences that are based on the land sector's specific challenges.

First, to ensure that the nuances of local legislation and practice are adequately captured, the main responsibility for the conduct of the exercise lies

Table 3.1   LGAF Dimensions, Ordered by Thematic Areas

THEMATIC AREA 1. LEGAL AND INSTITUTIONAL FRAMEWORK

LGI 1. Recognition of a continuum of rights. **The law recognizes a range of rights held by individuals as well as groups (including secondary rights as well as rights held by minorities and women).**

1   i   Existing legal framework recognizes rights held by most of the rural population, either through customary or statutory tenure regimes.

   ii   Existing legal framework recognizes rights held by most of the urban population, either through customary or statutory tenure regimes.

  iii   The tenure of most groups in rural areas is formally recognized, and clear regulations exist regarding groups' internal organization and legal representation.

  iv   Group tenure in informal urban areas is formally recognized, and clear regulations exist regarding the internal organization and legal representation of groups.

   v   The law provides opportunities for those holding land under customary, group, or collective tenure to fully or partially individualize land ownership and use. Procedures for doing so are affordable, clearly specified, safeguarded, and followed in practice.

LGI 2. Enforcement of rights. **The rights recognized by law are enforced (including secondary rights as well as rights of minorities and women).**

2   i   Most communal lands have boundaries demarcated and surveyed or mapped and communal rights registered.

   ii   Most individual properties in rural areas are formally registered.

  iii   Most individual properties in urban areas are formally registered.

  iv   A high percentage of land registered to physical persons is registered in the name of women, either individually or jointly.

   v   Common property under condominiums is recognized, and there are clear provisions in the law to establish arrangements for the management and maintenance of this common property.

  vi   When loss of rights occurs as a result of land use change not involving expropriation, compensation in cash or in kind is paid such that these people have comparable assets and can continue to maintain prior social and economic status.

(continued next page)

Table 3.1 (Continued)

LGI 3. *Mechanisms for recognition of rights.* The formal definition and assignment of rights, and process of recording of rights, accords with actual practice or, where it does not, provides affordable avenues for establishing such consistency in a nondiscriminatory manner.

3   i Nondocumentary forms of evidence are used alone to obtain full recognition of claims to property when other forms of evidence are not available.

     ii Legislation exists to formally recognize long-term, unchallenged possession and applies to both public and private land, although different rules may apply.

     iii The costs for first-time sporadic registration for a typical urban property is low compared to the property value.

     iv There are no informal fees that need to be paid to effect first registration.

     v The requirements for formalizing housing in urban areas are clear, straightforward, affordable, and implemented consistently in a transparent manner.

     vi There is a clear, practical process for the formal recognition of possession, and this process is implemented effectively, consistently, and transparently.

LGI 4. *Restrictions on rights.* Land rights are not conditional on adherence to unrealistic standards.

4   i There is a series of regulations regarding urban land use, ownership, and transferability that are for the most part justified on the basis of overall public interest and that are enforced.

     ii There is a series of regulations regarding rural land use, ownership, and transferability that are for the most part justified on the basis of overall public interest and that are enforced.

LGI 5. *Clarity of institutional mandates.* Institutional mandates concerning the regulation and management of the land sector are clearly defined, duplication of responsibilities is avoided, and information is shared as needed.

5   i There is a clear separation in the roles of policy formulation, implementation of policy through land management and administration, and the arbitration of any disputes that may arise as a result of implementation of policy.

     ii The mandated responsibilities exercised by the authorities dealing with land administration issues are clearly defined and nonoverlapping with those of other land sector agencies.

     iii Assignment of land-related responsibilities between the different levels of government is clear and nonoverlapping.

     iv Information related to rights in land is available to other institutions that need this information at reasonable cost and is readily accessible, largely because land information is maintained in a uniform way.

LGI 6. *Equity and nondiscrimination in the decision-making process.* Policies are formulated through a legitimate decision-making process that draws on inputs from all concerned. The legal framework is nondiscriminatory, and institutions to enforce property rights are equally accessible to all.

6   i A comprehensive policy exists or can be inferred by the existing legislation. Land policy decisions that affect sections of the community are based on consultation with those affected, and their feedback on the resulting policy is sought and incorporated in the resulting policy.

(continued next page)

Table 3.1 (Continued)

ii Land policies incorporate equity objectives that are regularly and meaningfully monitored, and their impact on equity issues is compared to that of other policy instruments.

iii Cost of implementation of land policy is estimated, expected benefits are identified and compared to cost, and there are sufficient budget, resources, and institutional capacity for implementation.

iv Land institutions report on land policy implementation in a regular, meaningful, and comprehensive way, with reports being publicly accessible.

THEMATIC AREA 2. LAND USE PLANNING, MANAGEMENT, AND TAXATION

LGI 7. Transparency of land use restrictions. **Changes in land use and management regulations are made in a transparent fashion and provide significant benefits for society in general rather than just for specific groups.**

7 i In urban areas, public input is sought in preparing and amending changes in land use plans, and the public responses are explicitly referenced in the report prepared by the public body responsible for preparing the new public plans. This report is publicly accessible.

ii In rural areas, public input is sought in preparing and amending land use plans, and the public responses are explicitly referenced in the report prepared by the public body responsible for preparing the new public plans. This report is publicly accessible.

iii Mechanisms to allow the public to capture a significant share of the gains from changing land use are regularly used and applied transparently based on clear regulation.

iv Most land that has had a change in land use assignment in the past 3 years has changed to the destined use.

LGI 8. Efficiency in the land use planning process. **Land use plans and regulations are justified, are effectively implemented, do not drive large parts of the population into informality, and are able to cope with population growth.**

8 i In the largest city in the country, urban development is controlled effectively by a hierarchy of regional and detailed land use plans that are kept up to date.

ii In the four major cities, urban development is controlled effectively by a hierarchy of regional and detailed land use plans that are kept up to date.

iii In the largest city in the country, the urban planning process or authority is able to cope with the increasing demand for serviced units and land as evidenced by the fact that almost all new dwellings are formal.

iv Existing requirements for residential plot sizes are met in most plots.

v The share of land set aside for specific use that is used for a nonspecified purpose in contravention of existing regulations is low.

LGI 9. Speed and predictability of applications for restricted land uses. **Development permits are granted promptly and predictably.**

9 i Requirements to obtain a building permit are technically justified, affordable, and clearly disseminated.

ii All applications for building permits receive a decision in a short period.

(continued next page)

Table 3.1   (Continued)

LGI-10. Transparency of valuations. **Valuations for tax purposes are based on clear principles, applied uniformly, updated regularly, and publicly accessible.**

10   i   The assessment of land and property values for tax purposes is based on market prices with minimal differences between recorded values and market prices across different uses and types of users, and valuation rolls are regularly updated.

ii   There is a policy that valuation rolls be publicly accessible, and this policy is effective for all properties that are considered for taxation.

LGI 11. Tax collection efficiency. **Resources from land and property taxes are collected, and the yield from land taxes exceeds the cost of collection.**

11   i   There are limited exemptions to the payment of land and property taxes, and the exemptions that exist are clearly based on equity or efficiency grounds and applied in a transparent and consistent manner.

ii   Most property holders liable for land and property tax are listed on the tax roll.

iii   Most assessed property taxes are collected.

iv   The amount of property taxes collected exceeds the cost of staff in charge of collection by a factor of more than 5.

THEMATIC AREA 3. MANAGEMENT OF PUBLIC LAND

LGI 12. Identification and clear management of public land. **Public land ownership is justified, inventoried, and under clear management responsibilities, and relevant information is publicly accessible.**

12   i   Public land ownership is justified by the provision of public goods at the appropriate level of government, and such land is managed in a transparent and effective way.

ii   The majority of public land is clearly identified on the ground or on maps.

iii   The management responsibility for different types of public land is unambiguously assigned.

iv   There are adequate budgets and human resources that ensure responsible management of public lands.

v   All the information in the public land inventory is accessible to the public.

vi   Key information for land concessions is recorded and publicly accessible.

LGI 13. Justification and time-efficiency of expropriation processes. **The state expropriates land only for overall public interest, and this is done efficiently.**

13   i   A minimal amount of land expropriated in the past 3 years is used for private purposes.

ii   The majority of land that has been expropriated in the past 3 years has been transferred to its destined use.

LGI 14. Transparency and fairness of expropriation procedures. **Expropriation procedures are clear and transparent, and compensation in kind or at market values is paid fairly and expeditiously.**

14   i   Where property is expropriated, fair compensation, in kind or in cash, is paid so that the displaced households have comparable assets and can continue to maintain prior social and economic status.

(continued next page)

Table 3.1   (Continued)

ii Fair compensation, in kind or in cash, is paid to all those with rights in expropriated land regardless of the registration status.

iii Most expropriated land owners receive compensation within one year.

iv Independent avenues to lodge a complaint against expropriation exist and are easily accessible.

v A first-instance decision has been reached for the majority of complaints about expropriation lodged during the past 3 years.

***LGI 15. Allocation of public land is transparent.* Transfer of public land to private use follows a clear, transparent, and competitive process, and payments are collected and audited.**

15 i Most public land disposed of in the past 3 years is through sale or lease through public auction or open tender process.

ii A majority of the total agreed-upon payments are collected from private parties on the lease of public lands.

iii All types of public land are generally divested at market prices in a transparent process irrespective of the investor's status (for example, domestic or foreign).

THEMATIC AREA 4. PUBLIC PROVISION OF LAND INFORMATION

***LGI 16. Completeness.* The land registry provides information on different private tenure categories in a way that is geographically complete and searchable by parcel as well as by right holder and can be obtained expeditiously by all interested parties.**

16 i Most records for privately held land registered in the registry are readily identifiable in maps in the registry or cadastre.

ii Relevant private encumbrances are recorded consistently and in a reliable fashion and can be verified at low cost by any interested party.

iii Relevant public restrictions or charges are recorded consistently and in a reliable fashion and can be verified at a low cost by any interested party.

iv The records in the registry can be searched by both right-holder name and parcel.

v Copies or extracts of documents recording rights in property can be obtained by anyone who pays the necessary formal fee, if any.

vi Copies or extracts of documents recording rights in property can generally be obtained within one day of request.

***LGI 17. Reliability.* Registry information is updated and sufficient to make meaningful inferences on ownership.**

17 i There are meaningful published service standards, and the registry actively monitors its performance against these standards.

ii Most ownership information in the registry or cadastre is up to date.

***LGI 18. Cost-effectiveness, accessibility, and sustainability.* Land administration services are provided in a cost-effective manner.**

18 i The cost for registering a property transfer is minimal compared to the property value.

ii The total fees collected by the registry exceed the total registry operating costs.

iii There is significant investment in capital in the system to record rights in land so that the system is sustainable but still accessible by the poor.

(continued next page)

Table 3.1 (Continued)

LGI 19. Transparency. Fees are determined and collected in a transparent manner.

19   i   A clear schedule of fees for different services is publicly accessible, and receipts are issued for all transactions.

     ii   Mechanisms to detect and deal with illegal staff behavior exist in all registry offices, and all cases are promptly dealt with.

THEMATIC AREA 5. DISPUTE RESOLUTION AND CONFLICT MANAGEMENT

LGI 20. Assignment of responsibility. Responsibility for conflict management at different levels is clearly assigned, in line with actual practice; relevant bodies are competent in applicable legal matters; and decisions can be appealed.

20   i   Institutions for providing a first instance of conflict resolution are accessible at the local level in the majority of communities.

     ii   There is an informal or community-based system that resolves disputes in an equitable manner, and decisions made by this system have some recognition in the formal judicial or administrative dispute resolution system.

     iii   There are no parallel avenues for conflict resolution or, if parallel avenues exist, responsibilities are clearly assigned and widely known, and explicit rules for shifting from one to the other are in place to minimize the scope for forum shopping.

     iv   A process and mechanism exist to appeal rulings on land cases at reasonable cost, with disputes resolved in a timely manner.

LGI 21. Low level of pending conflict. The share of land affected by pending conflicts is low and decreasing.

21   i   Land disputes in the formal court system are low compared to the total number of court cases.

     ii   A decision in a land-related conflict is reached in the first-instance court within 1 year in the majority of cases.

     iii   Long-standing land conflicts are a small proportion of the total pending land dispute court cases.

---

with a country coordinator who is a local expert in law or land administration. This person is critical to the success of the exercise and must be well qualified and carefully chosen. His or her responsibilities include the compilation of relevant background studies to be made available to those who will actually rate indicators as described later.

Second, dimensions to be rated are grouped into sets of about 10 topics. Panels are then formed, with three to five members who have experience with the relevant topic. The panels create consensus ratings for the indicators in their area by drawing on their own experiences, conducting informal interviews with experts, and using background information provided to them by the experts through the country coordinator.

Third, the intention of the LGAF is not to aggregate across indicators to create an overall score of land governance or of individual thematic areas. Such an aggregation does not seem to be warranted and would needlessly raise methodological questions regarding both the arbitrariness of weights for the aggregation and the interpretation and comparability of the aggregate score. In fact, the LGAF is not intended to be used as a scoring tool per se but rather as a tool to guide discussion about assessments from individual dimensions and drawing of lessons from good practice in different countries.

Finally, in contrast to the PEFA assessment tool, which is commonly applied during a two-week mission by a joint government-donor team that may be dominated by expatriates, the LGAF is applied over a three- to five-month period under the guidance of a local coordinator. The structured process involves assembly of relevant background information on key aspects of land governance. That phase of assembly is followed by meetings of diverse groups of stakeholders with firsthand knowledge or experience of the issues at stake to create a consensus rating and elaboration of a country report. This second phase helps obtain more in-depth background information and capture regional differences and local realities as perceived by different local stakeholder groups, thereby getting buy-in beyond the government and the donor community. The whole process is described in detail in the LGAF implementation manual, which, together with detailed country reports from the pilot cases, can be found online. The principal steps are summarized below.

COMPILATION OF BACKGROUND INFORMATION

In an area as complex and potentially controversial as land tenure, any exercise not based on rigorous review of available information and analysis is likely to be challenged. It is thus critical that ratings be based on a proper understanding of the underlying issues and that all participants begin with the same base of information. To accomplish this, the country coordinator, with assistance from a legal expert, puts together a "tenure typology" that is intended to provide an exhaustive listing of the legally recognized tenure types in the country, ideally providing the total land area under each category and the number of involved land holders and describing policy issues that are likely to arise. In addition, the coordinator recruits one local specialist for each of the following areas: land tenure, land use policy, public land management, and land administration. These specialists are tasked with putting together relevant studies and administrative or unofficial data to be obtained through personal contacts or phone calls to the relevant institutions. These data are documented and used as a basis for a subjective rating of the set of LGAF dimensions corresponding to the specialists' area of expertise, together with a justification for the ratings. Tenure typology, expert ratings, and a summary of the justifications provided by the experts serve as an input into the determination of the consensus rating for each of the dimensions.

Although the systematic involvement of experts as detailed above may be a significant improvement, issues such as the currency of registries; extent of female rights; collection of taxes; adherence to rules in case of expropriation;

transparency of public land dispositions; and nature, area, and age of disputes are nearly impossible to assess with any degree of confidence, even for individuals who are very familiar with a country's land tenure system, partly because they are likely to vary significantly across regions or localities. Though expert opinion may provide a general order of magnitude, making inferences on the basis of interregional or intertemporal variation in these issues makes reliance on hard data mandatory.

For demonstration of the feasibility and usefulness of having such data available, small surveys of key issues were undertaken in most pilot countries. Although samples were too small to approach representativeness, the exercise confirmed that, given their variation even within a country, such indicators are very meaningful and that their collection does not pose any conceptual difficulties. In fact, combining such data with other administrative data (for example, costs of service provision) or with socioeconomic information at the district level (for example, data on levels of poverty) will provide opportunities for making inferences about the outreach, client responsiveness, and potential poverty impact of land administration services and the cost effectiveness with which they are provided. Because such data refer to administrative functions that are performed routinely by different parts of the land administration system, their collection could easily be built into existing business processes. In light of this, however, spending significant resources on a separate data collection effort in the context of LGAF application is not cost-effective. A clear recommendation from the pilot country experiences, which is discussed later, is that collection and publication of such data on a routine basis should be part of any future donor efforts in regard to land administration systems.

EXPERT PANELS

Though systematic collection of information before any rating is undertaken is an important innovation by the LGAF, the core approach is to provide ratings through panels of experts, each including a diverse set of individuals who are exposed to different aspects of services in the explored area. Panel members typically include lawyers, academics, members of business chambers, bankers, representatives of nongovernmental organizations, government officials, land professionals, and others (for example, builders requiring permits) who interact with relevant institutions and, thus, have an empirical basis to assess performance. Experience suggests that three to five members can be selected for each of these panels and be provided with a small honorarium for their participation. They will bring together a variety of user perspectives and substantive expertise needed to provide a meaningful rating. For assurance that panel members assess only areas they are familiar with and to prevent overload, the 80 dimensions are distributed among seven panels on (a) land tenure;

(b) urban land use, planning, and development; (c) rural land use and policy; (d) land valuation and taxation; (e) public land management; (f) public provision of land information; and (g) dispute resolution.

In terms of process, to provide the basis for a meaningful discussion, panel members are briefed by the country coordinator on the objectives of the exercise, provided with the background material previously assembled, and asked to provide any additional information that might be relevant to the topic. This informal briefing (which often also entails a meeting) is then followed by the panel gathering in a workshop-like setting for a period ranging from a few hours to an entire day (for each panel), depending on the amount of prior preparation. The purpose of this meeting is to jointly discuss and review the material prepared; to add specific cases and experience; and, on this basis, to create a panel consensus rating through debate and aggregation of individual members' proposed scores.[2]

One advantage of this approach is that, on the basis of their experience in the sector, panel members will in many instances be able not only to identify cases of good or inadequate performance, but also to identify reasons leading to such performance. In the case of good performance, this approach can hold lessons for other countries. If performance is unsatisfactory, experts will be able either to point to policy changes or to identify issues that will need to be studied in more detail to provide a sound basis for policy recommendations. Using the discussion in the various panels, the country coordinator can then identify a prioritized list of policy interventions and gaps in available evidence in selected areas that can serve as a basis for recommendations to improve land governance, thereby making the exercise highly constructive.

To accomplish this list, the country coordinator summarizes results from the panel discussion in an aide-mémoire that is made available to all participants for review and approval. Aide-mémoires from the seven panel sessions provide the basis for, and are annexed to, a country report, the compilation of which is the responsibility of the country coordinator. The country report thus consists of three elements: (a) the land tenure typology; (b) the consensus rating arrived at for each of the dimensions, together with a summary of the evidence and materials used to create a consensus rating by the panels; and (c) priority recommendations for policy and areas where more evidence might be needed.

A CROSS-SECTORAL AND PARTICIPATORY APPROACH: INTEGRATING LGAF INTO THE POLICY PROCESS

A key characteristic of the LGAF that distinguishes it from other existing tools to assess land governance is that it is broad based and multidisciplinary, involving a diversity of themes and mobilized expertise. It is able to provide a synoptic view of land governance that cuts across sectors, institutions, and stakeholders. Moreover, the pilots showed that beyond the technical aspect, it could have some effect on policy design and adhesion to policy objectives by the different stakeholders. The LGAF methodology enables a participatory implementation that can raise awareness of the importance of using indicators to diagnose and track progress in land governance in the future, as well as provide inputs into land policy and reforms. For avoidance of criticism that could hinder the implementation of the tool, shed suspicion on its findings, and prevent the incorporation of findings into the land reform agenda, local buy-in is thus necessary. In this respect, it is important to note that rather than being a World Bank assessment made by outside experts, the LGAF is a tool that enables a consensual assessment made by legitimate local experts according to a well-defined and standardized methodology.

The choice of the country coordinator is thus crucial to ensure policy dialogue and incorporation of the results into the land reform agenda. Country coordinators must be recognized experts who are independent from government and vested interest groups while possessing an established network within the administration, among policy makers, and within civil society. During the pilots, some country coordinators organized informal workshops or participated in formal workshops to help inform the policy dialogue.

Linking LGAF to broader regional or global processes and the ability to implement it in parallel with ongoing reforms in a way that incorporates key officials in the panels helps to obtain buy-in, to access relevant information, and to affect policy. Working with existing institutions aiming to monitor land sector performance and policies could also be very useful avenues for implementing the LGAF. This includes working through land observatories, which several countries have established or envision creating.[3] Through an initiative spearheaded by the African Union, the Economic Commission of Africa, and the African Development Bank, African heads of state adopted a Framework and Guidelines for Land Policy in Africa. In this document, signatory states commit to tracking the progress in land policy implementation. The LGAF can help in fulfilling this commitment and could be a useful tool at their disposal.

There are many ways in which the LGAF implementation can be made more participatory, and debate of the background information and follow-up actions can be encouraged. At the country level, a website could be used to identify and document expertise, to facilitate collection of data, and to exchange information and experiences. Identifying countries with high scores can then help to identify and disseminate global best practice, to compare lessons, and to build capacity in a way that involves all stakeholders. A website can also serve as a repository of relevant methodological and substantial information to help country coordinators manage the different

Although the pilot applications of the LGAF were intended primarily to demonstrate the feasibility of a tool to assess and monitor land governance, they also illustrated the value of the tool to help with policy dialogue in three dimensions:

■ *Policy analysis.* Given its broad scope, the LGAF offers the possibility of a participatory, consensual, and comprehensive diagnostic of land issues cutting across traditional sectors. Adherence to the process by policy makers makes it a suitable and credible tool to structure and organize the policy dialogue. This tool can help to identify areas where more in-depth study will be needed. Moreover, the structured approach allows the user to identify global best practice in each of the areas covered by the LGAF, providing important inputs to local policy makers who often were unaware of, and thus could learn from, ways in which change was achieved in other countries.

■ *Operational and project work.* In addition to providing a relatively quick and low-cost assessment of needs in the land sector, which could then possibly be addressed by specific operations, the LGAF also can help to clarify the objectives of projects, the complementary areas of policy that need to be addressed, and the way in which outputs can be measured and recorded. In this respect, a number of bilateral agencies have expressed interest in using the approach as a part of project preparation, making use of the LGAF as the project objectives are gradually identified.

■ *Risk mitigation.* One of the main reasons land is traditionally considered high risk is because land policy can affect development outcomes in diverse and often unexpected ways. Having a tool that allows investors to monitor these risks in key areas will be increasingly important for partners' ability to support this sector and, thus, unlock the potential of very large and long-term development.

phases of the implementation and to provide a platform for online comment and discussion to ensure that background information is complete and accurate and to monitor implementation of policy recommendations.

NOTES

1. PEFA is a partnership between the World Bank, the European Commission, the United Kingdom's Department for International Development, the Swiss State Secretariat for Economic Affairs, the French Ministry of Foreign Affairs, the Royal Norwegian Ministry of Foreign Affairs, and the International Monetary Fund that aims to support integrated and harmonized approaches to assessment and reform

in public expenditure, procurement, and financial accountability. It aims to strengthen recipient and donor ability (a) to assess the condition of country public expenditure, procurement, and financial accountability systems and (b) to develop a practical sequence of reform and capacity-building actions, in a manner that encourages country ownership, reduces the transaction costs to countries, enhances donor harmonization, allows monitoring of progress of country public finance management performance over time, better addresses developmental and fiduciary concerns, and leads to improved effect of reforms. The partnership began in 2001, and since finalization of the assessment framework in 2005, it has conducted 127 assessments in 105 countries. See Public Expenditure and Financial Accountability, http://www.pefa.org.

2. Procedures varied slightly across pilot countries, partly in response to local practices and country coordinator characteristics. This experience indicates that the most effective approach will be to provide written information to panel members together with the invitation for a first meeting to explain the general methodology; to present the results (including the preliminary scores) from the expert investigation; and to ask panel members to identify sources of additional information, which the country coordinator can collect in advance of a second meeting. Results from this approach, together with a tentative policy recommendation, if circulated in advance, will then provide a basis for panel members to have a meaningful discussion that will allow them to create a consensus view (or note any dissenting views) during a second meeting. In this way, this aide-mémoire can evolve over time and be reviewed by panel members more than once. Providing an honorarium for such efforts is appropriate to compensate panel members for the time spent, to help equalize input across members, and to ensure accountability for results.

3. Madagascar is one example (see the website http://www.observatoire-foncier.mg, which regularly publishes analyses of ongoing land policies).

REFERENCE

World Bank. Forthcoming. "Benin: Sustainable Options for Agricultural Diversification." Report 54495-BJ, section on Securing Land Rights for Improved Productivity of Agriculture, World Bank, Washington, DC.

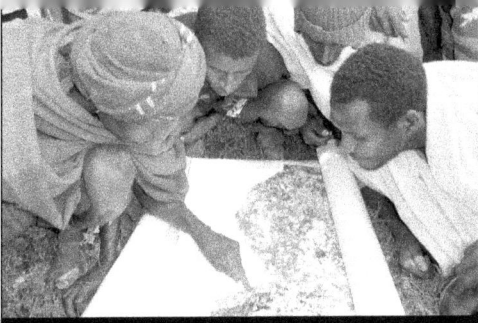

CHAPTER FOUR

Applying the Land
Governance Assessment
Framework in Practice:
Evidence from Five
Pilot Cases

evelopment of a tool to apply the framework in practice required an
iterative and adaptive process. To allow such a process, five countries
with very diverse institutional and socioeconomic backgrounds—Peru,
the Kyrgyz Republic, Tanzania, Ethiopia, and Indonesia—were selected for pilot
testing. The discussion and cross-country interaction facilitated by this process
was crucial to improve the framework and to ensure that it will be adapted for a
range of contexts. Because pilot cases aimed to help develop the methodology,
not all of them are fully consistent with the final framework. This notwithstanding, it was felt that there is considerable value in including the main results from
each country case study in this report to illustrate the potential usefulness of the
approach and the results that can be expected. For each case, we provide a brief
justification of country choice, a summary of the tenure typology, some highlights from the discussion of individual areas of the assessment, and a number of
priority recommendations for policy that emerged in the process.

PERU

In recent years, Peru has experienced rapid and relatively robust economic
growth (9.8 percent in 2008) that some observers attribute to strong private

investment following two decades of policies in pursuit of microeconomic stability and extension of legal property rights to more Peruvians. As a result of such policies, most of Peru's land legislation seems adequate or progressive, offering lessons in areas such as expropriation, transfer of state land to private investors, recognition of group rights, and systematic first-time registration of rights. At the same time, proper implementation of land sector regulations and policies is made more urgent by a number of recent developments:

- *Rapid urban expansion.* The massive growth of informal human settlements and urbanization that shaped the growth of Peru's major cities since the 1960s has contributed to a boom in the formal construction sector. The expansion of this sector has driven job creation and growth while spawning a new middle class. However, the hierarchy of planning instruments established by law to help organize and control development has not been implemented fully, and in the few jurisdictions that have formulated plans, those plans have quickly become outdated. Moreover, the best plans focus on the nation's largest cities and a few affluent municipalities. In Lima, which is home to one-third of Peru's population, the formal development plan dates back to 1992 and has been updated only in an ad hoc manner, mainly in reaction to economic and political pressures. This situation suggests a need to plan in a way that is more orderly than the waves of occupation and ex post regularization of the past.

- *A rise in demand for land from local or foreign investors.* Demand for new land is boosted by three factors: (a) the development of nontraditional agriculture (for example, asparagus, for which Peru is now the world's top exporter) mainly on the coast, where investment projects aim to expand agriculture areas through irrigation; (b) the attractiveness of natural resources such as lumber and gas and of areas with potential to develop agroindustrial crops, biofuels, and environmental services (for example, organic produce, ecocertified wood, and ecotourism) in the Peruvian Amazon; and (c) mining commodities, such as gold, copper, and zinc in the Andean Sierra. To prevent this demand from giving rise to conflict between local communities and investors, policies must recognize and protect local land rights so that investment is based on negotiation with existing users.

- *A movement toward decentralization.* Though decentralization created major opportunities for increased access to services, which necessitated maintenance of registries in a cost-effective manner, it also multiplied the number of players in the sector.[1] Unless policy is laid out clearly and is based on a legitimate process and the fulfillment of overall objectives is regularly checked using empirical data, a danger exists that ideologically driven disparate visions and conflicting ad hoc agendas will increase coordination costs and, thus, jeopardize long-term development. This possibility suggests a need for democratic processes of policy making that are cognizant of the trade-offs involved, for clear formulation of policy, and for monitoring of implementation on objective empirical information.

Recognition and Enforcement of Rights

Peruvian law recognizes property rights for most situations encountered in Peru, either at the individual or group level. In urban areas, the law (Law 26687), recognizes different types of informal tenure (such as squatter settlements, as well as housing associations and cooperatives that legally bought agricultural land but developed it without complying with urban planning regulations) and informal land development in traditional unplanned towns (*centros poblados* and *pueblos tradicionales*). The law also defines requirements and procedures for formalization. In rural areas, the land rights of Andean peasant farming communities and native Amazonian indigenous communities are recognized, and rules for demarcation and titling of their territories have been established. Regulations contain provisions regarding the internal organization and representation of communities. (See Law 24656, recognizing peasant farming communities;[2] Law 24657, regarding the demarcation and titling of community territories;[3] Law 26845, regarding land titling of peasant farming communities on coastal areas;[4] and Law 22175, regarding native communities and development of the Amazon.[5]) On the basis of these laws, some 70 percent of properties in urban and rural areas received ownership titles. As presented in more detail in the tenure typology (see table 4.1), this percentage corresponds to 7.2 million titled parcels hosting almost 23 million people (out of a population of 29 million). In urban areas, 14 million people are estimated to live on titled properties, and 6 million live on individual properties not supported by titles. In rural areas, 3.9 million people live on titled individual property on private land, whereas 1.5 million live on untitled individual property on state or private land. Also, 5,055 peasant farming communities out of 6,082 on some 23 million hectares (ha) and 1,262 native communities in the Peruvian Amazon out of 1,444 have been provided titles to their land. This represents an additional 4.5 million people living on titled land.[6]

The law has adequate provision to facilitate large-scale formalization. It recognizes the legitimacy of past undisputed occupation in regularization processes through "nondocumentary" (unwritten) forms of evidence.[7] It is also advanced in recognizing women's rights. Mass-formalization campaigns include community meetings to provide information about women's rights, formalization brigades are trained to check for absent spouses in cases of males claiming to be single household heads, and registration procedures include safeguards for rights of spouses.[8] As a result, the Commission for the Formalization of Informal Property (Organismo de Formalización de la Propiedad Informal [COFOPRI]), the titling agency, reports that 53.5 percent of urban titles and 51.1 percent of rural titles have been issued to women, either individually or jointly.

Table 4.1 Tenure Typology for Peru

Tenure type	Area and population[a]	Legal recognition and characteristics	Overlaps and potential issues
Urban sector			
Titled private individual property in developed areas (including property formalized by COFOPRI)	Area: 53,600 ha (conventional formal property: 19,000 ha; COFOPRI: 34,000 ha) Population: 14.8 million Parcels: 3.5 million (conventional formal property: 1.1 million; COFOPRI: 2.4 million)	Legal recognition: Civil Code Registration/recording: Registered Transferability: Transferable with no restrictions	Overlap can occur between traditional formal owners in peri-urban areas if cadastre information is deficient. Not applicable to COFOPRI-formalized property.
Individual property not supported by property titles in peri-urban squatter settlements on public land, housing programs, and other categories of informal settlements	Area: 29,100 ha Population: 6.5 million Parcels: 1.6 million	Legal recognition: COFOPRI regulations; Law 26687 Registration/recording: Eligible for registration after completing formalization Transferability: Possessory rights typically transferred informally by settlers	Overlap can occur with state property and in some cases with private properties.
Informal urban centers described as *centros poblados* and *pueblos tradicionales*: groups of city blocks and street layouts not creating an urban development and partially finished construction on housing lots directly and individually purchased by each member of the informal urban area		Legal recognition: COFOPRI regulations; Law 26687 Registration/recording: Eligible for registration Transferability: Possessory rights typically transferred informally by settlers	Some overlap occurs with private property rights (individual owners, owner associations, peasant farming communities).

Category	Legal status	Area / Population	Observations
Unregistered popular housing developments (cooperatives, associations, and other types of housing associations)	Legal recognition: COFOPRI regulations; Law 26687 Registration/recording: Eligible for registration Transferability: Legally transferrable but unable to be registered		Some overlap occurs with private property rights (individual owners, owner associations, peasant farmer communities).

Rural sector

Category	Legal status	Area / Population	Observations
Titled individual property	Legal recognition: Civil Code Registration/recording: Registered Transferability: Transferable	Area: 6.5 million ha Population: 3.9 million Parcels: 2.0 million	Rights on individual rural property without cadastral support (that is, not resulting from formalization but derived from old transfers) typically overlap with other rights.
Untitled individual property on private land	Legal recognition: Legislative Decrees 667 and 1089 Registration: Eligible for registration once formalized Transferability: Possession transferred informally	Area: 3.3 million ha Population: 1.5 million Parcels: 1.0 million	Private rights exist, whether registered or not. It is much more difficult to formalize occupation of private land than occupation of public land.
Untitled individual property on state land	Legal recognition: Legislative Decree 1089 Registration: Eligible for registration after formalization Transferability: Possession transferred informally		Occupation of state land required for public purposes. Occupation of land dedicated to archeological sites or found to be unsafe cannot be regularized.
Andean and coastal peasant farming communities (comunidades campesinas)	Legal recognition: Law 24656—Peasant farmer communities; Law 24657—Community Territories' Demarcation and Titling; Legislative Decree 1064—Juridical Regime for Use of Agricultural Land; Law 26845—Titling of Coastal Communities' Land Registration: Eligible for registration; some registered	Titled communities: 5,055 Area: 23.2 million ha Population: 4.3 million Communities without a title: 1,027 Area: 4.7 million ha Population: Unknown	Communities registered before formalization programs were established lack a cadastre support. Rights frequently overlap those of other rights holders, including other communities, informal settlements, individuals, associations, and cooperatives.

(continued next page)

Table 4.1 (Continued)

Tenure type	Area and population[a]	Legal recognition and characteristics	Overlaps and potential issues
Amazonian indigenous native communities (*comunidades nativas*)	Titled communities: 1,262 Population: 209,600 Area: 10.8 million ha[b] Communities without a title: 182 Population: 123,375 Area: 1.3 million ha[c]	Transferability: Transferrable after agreement by the members of the community following stringent formalities Legal recognition: Law 22175—Native Communities and Jungle and High Jungle Development Registration: Eligible for registration; some registered Transferability: Transferable after agreement by the members of the community following stringent formalities	Frequent overlaps occur with other communities, informal settlements, and individual property rights.
Other groups, some using land under common property, others on individual tenure (*comuneros*, people who settle in hitherto unoccupied areas; *colonos*, migrants from Andean areas; and *ribereños*, people who settle on riverbanks)	Population: Unknown Area: Unknown (according to studies, *ribereños* occupy 4.1 million ha of forest)	Legal recognition: None Registration/recording: No Transferability: Transfers occurring extralegally	

Source: Various sources; compiled by V. Endo.

Note: COFOPRI = Organismo de Formalización de la Propiedad Informal; ha = hectare.

a. These figures are estimates based mainly on Peru's National Statistics Institute census and COFOPRI data, with assumptions regarding the percentage of formal properties in different zones. Details are available upon request. Some of the tenure categories presented in this table are defined by law. For urban areas, the law defines squatter settlements, informal urban centers (*pueblos tradicionales* and *centros urbanos informales*), and popular housing developments (*urbanizaciones populares, asociaciones,* and *cooperativas de vivienda*). For rural areas, the law defines individual property, communal property of peasant farmer communities in coastal and highland areas, and communal property of native communities in the Amazon Basin.

b. Among the titled native communities, 600 are registered without Universal Transverse Mercator coordinates, representing 4 million ha of land.

c. February 2009 figures from Peru's Institute for Well-Being (IBC) differ slightly. According to IBC, of the 1,509 native communities in Peru, 1,232 are titled and 277 are not. The 277 communities without a title represent 2.4 million ha. There are also 4 million ha of land without a title for six communities in a

The 1993 constitution cancelled restrictions on rights (for example, a former ban on corporate land ownership, plot size limits, and prohibition of certain types of land-related contracts) that had been established during the "land to the tiller" reforms of the 1960s and 1970s, suggesting that few restrictions on land persist,[9] and that the remaining restrictions on property rights are based on the broader public interest. In fact, the constitution states as an objective the increase of rural land productivity through the creation of a free market in land and the elimination of restrictions to ownership.

However, two main challenges remain to be addressed. First, without clear cut-off dates, large-scale land regularization—albeit regarded as successful as a national policy for securing tenure, reducing conflict, promoting citizenship, and creating economic opportunities—became an open-ended process that may encourage speculative land occupations and, thus, undermine existing property rights. In urban areas, governments have become used to extending deadlines for recognizing new groups to be able to add them to the formalization roster as new informal settlements spring up over time (often organized by slumlords). In rural areas, the focus on formalizing individual rights and the delays in dealing with the land rights of Andean and Amazonian communities have created acute problems because these circumstances led to the appearance of new "indigenous" groups claiming recognition. These groups include new generations of communities—such as *comuneros*, who settle in hitherto unoccupied areas; *ribereños*, who settle on riverbanks; and *colonos*, urban and rural migrants who are in search of opportunity—but also "communities" strategically placed through large companies and ambitious local entrepreneurs who use these communities as a front to gain access to valuable rights and to circumvent existing regulations. Speculators and private firms have "planted" settlers without traditional ties to the land in areas slated for public investment or where other private investors have been granted concessionary rights, or as part of a concerted strategy to deforest the area and then have it adjudicated as agricultural land. This situation poses significant legal challenges that have not yet been satisfactorily resolved.

Second, though the legal recognition of community rights is a positive first step, such rights can be defended or used as a basis to share in the benefits of land-related investment only if boundaries are demarcated on the ground and if there are mechanisms for intracommunity decision making as well as representation to the outside. Progress on mapping remains limited, especially in the Amazon, where a mere 85 native communities out of 1,510 have a formal digital map of their territories and instead rely on ambiguous mete and bounds descriptions.[10] Lack of boundary demarcation makes it impossible for communities to effectively exercise their rights, leading to numerous intercommunity conflicts and, more important, to disputes with settlers (*colonos*) who occupy community land. Legal loopholes allow the use of illegal logging and subsequent application for rezoning as a means to gain backdoor access to large tracts of land for agricultural production, a very serious issue that not only has led to overexploitation and irreversible loss of natural resources on a large scale, but also has created a large number of serious conflicts. Because formal requirements for representation are complex, communities face numerous obstacles to complying with the law to appoint representatives and enforce their agreements, something that further limits their ability to interact with the state. This situation has emerged as a major hurdle to completing the titling of the rest of the communities and as a key impediment to negotiating rights-of-way with private operators who need to cross native lands to reach their concessions. Private sector actors often complain about the absence of authorized representatives of communities ("We don't know who to talk to"), opportunistic behavior by self-appointed leaders, and the resulting inability to enforce agreements. Issues related to representation also affect the ability of communities to allow members to hold individual properties. Efforts are urgently needed to create awareness and mechanisms for implementing existing rules to prevent fraud and to ensure transparent decision making over fundamental issues such as the divestment of community land.

Policy and Institutional Framework

Although institutional mandates are defined in an unambiguous way, vertical overlaps arise in practice—partly as a result of Peru's transition to decentralization—owing to the complex distribution of roles among levels of government (central, regional, provincial, and district), legal voids, and poor skills in decentralized government agencies. For example, regional governments often are not ready to make decisions falling within their competence. Competition among agencies for scarce resources and disputes among political players further aggravate the situation. For example, in an effort to create a standardized, national mechanism for issuance of land development and building permits, the central government passed a regulation establishing a hierarchy of territorial plans to set rules and limits for urban land. Soon after, Lima's Metropolitan Municipality, invoking its autonomy to regulate territory planning, issued another regulation introducing specific rules within its jurisdiction, thus disregarding the national law.

Land-related policy making in Peru is often piecemeal and sector driven, lacking participation and transparency. Rather than stemming from a preexisting coherent vision, policies can emerge in an ad hoc way from public statements by the president or a minister, be included in legal provisions governing specific land administration areas,[11] or be addressed in a ministry's plans.[12] Such examples create a perception of policy making being top-down, with little consultation and often serving the interests of a narrow elite rather than the majority of the population.[13] In addition, little monitoring is done to ensure that policies, once adopted, have the desired effect (or that corrections are made in case they do not) and that equity concerns are addressed. Although agencies publish regular progress reports and are subject to transparency regulations, accomplishments are not measured against a baseline, and there are no established performance indicators or reporting and accountability requirements. Often, information reported by public agencies is not available to the public. Although equity goals are implicit or even explicit in many laws and regulations (for example, formalization rules granting direct benefits and free services to residents in urban and peasant settlements, as well as to Andean peasant farmers and to native communities in the Amazon), the lack of coherent policies for implementation have made it difficult, if not impossible, to attain those objectives. For example, the very modern services offered by the property registry are not accessible to many beneficiaries of formalization programs, who in turn are stepping back into informality. Failure to consistently monitor and publicize information on policy implementation makes it difficult to take action to ensure more coherent policy implementation.

Land Use Planning and Taxation

Urban planning in Peru reflects the country's high inequality. Although strict building controls and municipal oversight are difficult to evade in high-income districts, plans or controls are largely absent from low-income districts, where most buildings are erected without permits. Such uncontrolled development, while providing basic housing, has created major problems for supplying services, thereby contributing to environmental degradation, settlement of hazardous areas, and urban sprawl. In practice, urban planning is often poor. Provincial plans are outdated, and regional-level plans are typically too general. Apart from a few district municipalities in Lima (dubbed "the five ladies" in reference to their well-heeled residents) and a few more in the provinces, development plans are either nonexistent or outdated. Decisions on land use change, zoning, and building licenses are thus made on an ad hoc basis, leaving ample room for discretion. The causes for the disconnect between regulations on paper and the reality on the ground include accelerated urban growth, the inability of existing planning tools and institutions to anticipate and adapt, lack of national policies with a comprehensive view of land use, and disjointed interventions by government and private organizations in the land sector. For instance, the property formalization initiatives of COFOPRI are not coordinated with housing policies, which are enforced with total disregard for local governments' land use plans.[14]

Although models to determine property values for purposes of taxation are regularly updated, components of the formula used to calculate a building's value are based on political criteria rather than market values. No consideration is given to the building's economic use, so that a private house may have to pay higher taxes than a similar property for commercial purposes. Average taxpayers can rarely get access to the official gazette in which property tax schedules are published, reducing transparency. Tax breaks, although coherent overall and based on principles of equity and efficiency, are excessive and often just compensate for other distortions.[15] Peru also has a lack of infrastructure: 95 percent of its 1,834 municipalities lack a cadastre to manage collections.[16] Lack of transparency, together with limited provision of municipal services, makes tax collection difficult and prone to political argument.[17] As a result, the collection of property tax by local governments is estimated to be below 50 percent of potential in most Peruvian districts.

Management and Divestment of State-Owned Lands

In Peru, "state goods" may be in the public or the private domain.[18] The state is the default owner of properties over which there are no impending private, peasant, or native community rights. Management of state-owned lands is entrusted to the National State-Owned Goods System (*Sistema Nacional de Bienes Estatales*), mainly under the national government (executive, legislative, and judicial bodies, as well as independent agencies) and regional or local governments. The system is governed by the National Superintendency of State-Owned Goods (*Superintendencia Nacional de Bienes Estatales*), which issues regulations on the management of public land (including rentals and any form of divestiture) and oversees the purchase of state-owned goods. Public land is divested at market prices in a transparent process that is independent of the investor's status or nationality. Transfers of land from the state's private domain require a public auction in which the starting price for bidding is based on an assessment of the property's commercial value.[19] Buyers must pay in advance to ensure that the total payment from auctioned properties is collected. The state may also award concessions for development of renewable natural resources (for example, forests) and nonrenewable resources (for example, minerals) on public land (see box 4.1 for details on public land divestiture in Peru). Key information on land concessions (that is, the locality and area of the concession, the parties involved, and the financial terms of the concession) is recorded and is publicly available.

However, though public landholdings are justified by public interest, weak institutions hamper effective management. Squatters often occupy riverbanks, parks, and buffer zones. Although responsibilities for the management of state-owned goods are distributed among levels of government, and progress has been made in setting up a system for their effective management, more remains to be done. Indeed, less than 30 percent of public land is estimated to be clearly identified on the ground or on maps. Peru's state-owned goods inventory (*Sistema de Información Nacional de Bienes Estatales*) has been designed as a database to manage state-owned goods under the National Superintendency of State-Owned Goods, but progress toward building an inventory has been slow, partly because of the lack of registration of indigenous communities.

In an effort to uphold private land rights and to prevent government from abuse of power, constitutional rules tightly circumscribe cases in which expropriation can be used. Article 70 of the constitution stipulates that expropriations can be

Box 4.1 Divestment of State Land in Peru

Proinversión is Peru's national investment promotion agency, which assists decentralized levels of government in attracting investments. The mechanism used to divest public lands for investment projects depends on whether projects are initiated by the government or by an investor. If a government agency (a ministry or a regional or local government) has identified the desirability of carrying out a given project, it will request Proinversión to begin promoting the project. Proinversión will initiate a process of regularizing any land rights to determine the nature of preexisting claims that may need to be respected or cleared and the types of land rights that can be granted to the private investor. If illegitimate claims existed, they are cleared. If legitimate preexisting claims existed, they are treated following the rules for expropriation and compensation. The technical defects of the title are also cleared (for instance, if reference to a tract of public land is made in several records with poor descriptions, rectifications in the property registry will be made). The intention of divesting the land is then published in the official gazette, the local and international newspapers, and a government website. The terms of bidding (that is, minimum investment required and minimum bid price for the land) are published for a minimum of 90 days (longer if the project is more complex). Before any bids are accepted, bidders must prequalify by proving liquid assets to cover at least 60 percent of the minimum bid price and of the intended amount of investment on the land. For prequalified bidders, bids are assessed and ranked by offered price and the amount of projected investment. Monetary offers are then presented, and a winner is declared. Before the contract is signed, the land must be paid for, and a letter of credit covering the amount of the proposed investment must be deposited with the government.

If projects involving the divestiture of public land are at the initiative of private investors, a similar process is followed. In that case, the potential investor must present a detailed business plan that describes the amount of proposed investment and price for the land before a board comprising public and private sector specialists, including the responsible line ministries (especially the Ministry of Agriculture if irrigation is involved). If the proposed project is considered viable and not in conflict with existing regulations, the proposal is published for a minimum of 90 days to allow other potential investors to offer to carry out the project. If any investor comes forward, a public bidding process as described earlier will be initiated. If, during the 90-day publication period, nobody has shown interest in the project, the investor is allowed to proceed as originally proposed.

Source: Hernandez 2010.

carried out only for reasons of national security or "public need" (for example, to build a road or bridge whose beneficiaries could be anyone and not a specific class of individuals). The expropriations law clearly states that expropriations are void unless the state is the direct beneficiary.[20] Public scrutiny and debate of individual expropriations is ensured by the requirement that any case of expropriation must be authorized by congress in a law explicitly spelling out the future use of expropriated goods. To ensure an impartial and realistic valuation, property values must be determined in a court proceeding. Expropriated owners have the right to cash payment of the land's market value plus remedies for any damages. To avoid abuse, mandatory deadlines have been established as well. Expropriation orders will lapse automatically after 6 months if the judiciary process to assess values has not yet started and after 24 months if court proceedings are not yet concluded. Moreover, if within one year of the conclusion of the court process the expropriated property is not used for its planned purpose, it will automatically revert to the original owner.

Two potential issues with expropriation are worth mentioning. First, only registered owners or recognized occupants are eligible for remedies, although in practice (and to prevent costly delays), road construction companies often negotiate with and pay noneligible occupants even if they are not legally entitled to compensation.[21] Second, a controversial 2005 law interprets expropriation of private land squatted upon before December 2005 as being for "public need." Although not applied yet, this interpretation stirred up much debate and criticism, because contrary to prevailing interpretation, the concept of public need was stretched to include specific groups of citizens as beneficiaries—in this case, regularized private land squatters.

Public Provision of Land Information

The property registry is part of the National Public Registries System.[22] Since its establishment in 1994, the National Superintendency of Public Registries (SUNARP) made good progress in introducing technology and improving customer service. These improvements helped to eliminate petty corruption, to professionalize staff members who are now trained on a regular basis, to automate registration processes, and to cut delivery times through online service. However, users still find registration procedures slow and unpredictable.[23] The system protects registrars from political pressure by granting them autonomy in their decisions. However, the application of this principle, together with the lack of standardized requirements, results in discretionary interpretation of laws. It is exacerbated by the understaffing of city registration offices and the complexity of regulations governing transactions that are dispersed among the civil code and other nonstandardized and frequently changing laws, decrees, and regulations. Coordination with other institutions remains weak, and no standardized cadastral information is shared with other institutions.

Lack of a spatial reference also greatly reduces the value of registration. Traditionally, Peru's system of registration was textual only, and maps were added only when large-scale property formalization programs started in 1990. As a result, 57 percent of the approximately 9.5 million registered properties are estimated to lack a spatial reference. In addition to possibly undermining confidence in the registry, this deficiency reduces the value of registration in two ways: (a) it does little to eliminate increasing levels of boundary disputes in rural and peri-urban areas, where land values are increasing, and (b) allowing information to be retrieved using only the owner's name makes it difficult for prospective buyers, renters, or lenders to use the registry as an instrument to promote the real estate and financial market. A program to add spatial references to these textual records is currently under way. To address the lack of spatial reference and ensuing boundary conflicts, SUNARP has set up cadastre units specifically devoted to checking rights overlaps, and cadastre offices are preparing mosaics of existing registration dockets for which no maps are available.[24]

Although relevant registry information (liens and encumbrances) is available, the cost of accessing it is high. The main source of this cost is the need to hire professional services as a result of a court decision that users must check registration records as well as the title deeds supporting them. Registry information is also not sufficiently up to date. Because inscription in the property registry is voluntary, the high cost of formalizing property transactions and the lack of a "registration culture" all reduce updating, with compliance varying with property value and wealth. Field sampling in Chiclayo, Cusco, and Lima revealed that the information was up to date for 81 percent of the most valuable properties but for only 60 percent of the poorest ones. If one assumes that the latter correspond to the settlements formalized by COFOPRI, which has been in campaign mode over the past 13 years, this comparison would suggest a rate of reversion to informality of 40 percent of recently formalized properties.

Since 1994, public registry modernization promoted by SUNARP has led to significant improvements in transparency. Rate schedules are fixed and published in all offices. Registrars are required to account for the rates they apply to individual cases, and registry office managers continuously evaluate performance and service quality. To fight corruption and to prevent users from choosing the registrar to process their files, an electronic system distributes files among registrars. However, the long-term sustainability of the registry could be limited, because most decentralized offices are not financially sustainable. The six largest offices in large cities cross-subsidize operations in the remainder, where limited demand constrains the potential revenue base. It is noticeable that no public registry exists in 131 (out of 194) provinces throughout Peru, suggesting that some users must incur higher costs for accessing services.

Dispute Resolution

Legal pluralism is enshrined in Peru's constitution. The formal system comprises the judiciary; COFOPRI's property administrative court; the courts of the public registries; and other government agencies in charge of providing land administration functions, such as municipalities' land regulators. As long as they do not breach fundamental rights, Andean peasant and Amazonian indigenous communities perform judicial functions following customary law within their territories, and the formal system is mandated to uphold such decisions. Informal but legitimate and recognized justice institutions, including community assemblies, peasants' civil squads (*rondas campesinas*), city civil squads (*rondas urbanas*), and "neighborhood presidents," play an important role in administering justice for the roughly 50 percent of the population who live too far from departmental capitals where formal justice systems are located to make access to these systems a viable option. Crimes or faults within a community's jurisdiction may be tried in compliance with internal law; the state's courts have a mandate to acknowledge those decisions.

However, although the informal or community-based system resolves disputes in an equitable manner, its verdicts have little recognition in the formal judicial or administrative dispute resolution system, because professional judges do not acknowledge decisions from community authorities. Moreover, because people know that the formal system may not acknowledge community court decisions, they opt for the local justice of the peace or a combined court. If a conflict is settled in a peasant or native community, for example, and the losing party is not satisfied with the verdict, the latter may resort to the formal judiciary, disregarding the decision of community authorities. The organization of formal justice is also problematic, because lack of a centralized information system creates an opportunity for forum shopping by parties and parallel pursuit of proceedings, including manipulations to identify a judge that will best fit their interests.

Policy Recommendations

Policy recommendations for Peru cover the necessity to improve equity in land administration, to continue the process of formalizing property rights in urban and rural areas, to make decentralization more effective, and to ensure that land policy achievement are sustainable.

Improved Equity in Land Administration

Although legal provisions for land administration are largely appropriate, capacity gaps, lack of resources, and institutional fragmentation prevent full implementation and effectiveness of such provisions while creating an impression of a system that, although well designed, serves the needs of the rich while bypassing the poor and the vulnerable. For example, property registries that include Web-based services are available to the educated and residents of provincial capitals, where registration offices operate, but not the poor, who lack awareness and, given the high transaction costs, the resources to access the system. Efforts to secure property rights may be seen not only to bypass the marginalized, but also actually to increase their vulnerability, especially for Amazonian indigenous communities, which are subject to pressures from neighbors, *colonos*, private investors, and land speculators. Similarly, provisions for land use planning and property tax collection are operational in most affluent areas but are out of reach for most local governments. A key consideration is that land policies must bring together the efforts of land management agencies operating at various levels of government. Such effort should be joined not just by central, regional, and local government agencies, but also by land governance experts, academics, and civil society organizations.

Completed Formalization of Property Rights in Urban and Rural Areas

For urban areas, continued extension of deadlines for formalization—a favored government response so far—will increase incentives for new invasions, play into the hands of informal developers, and be socially inefficient.[25] Encouraging new housing strategies for the neediest Peruvians seems a more efficient and peaceful way to provide adequate, safe housing to the poor. For example, instead of the typical public housing programs, which offer brand-new homes reachable only by the middle classes, funds for densification of already formalized settlements could allow individual title holders to receive credit to build second-floor apartments for rental or sale in areas where public services are available. Planning new settlements for progressive development, that is, offering plots with services and minimum infrastructure rather than finished housing, may be less effective as a political advertisement but better for the poor than the current pattern of invasions by speculators, resistance to eviction, and long waits for infrastructure and service provision.

In rural areas, enforcing the rights of Andean peasant and Amazonian native communities requires acting quickly to formalize their land rights, clearly defining the boundaries of their territories, and improving the representation of these groups with the outside. To that end, an important step is to ascertain whether existing land tenure types (*comunidades campesinas* and *comunidades nativas*, legally defined in terms of their historical and ethnic bonds to the land) are sufficient to capture the dynamic realities of the rural areas or, if they do not, to devise new types. For assurance that progress is achieved and monitored, one suggestion is to create, within COFOPRI, indicators about the remaining demand for formalization according to land tenure type and to then monitor progress over time in coordination with local governments.

Effective Decentralization

To make decentralization effective, to assist poor municipalities in building capacity to collect property tax (including mechanisms for service provision to make tax collection legitimate), to update land assessments, and to correctly provide tax breaks to poor households can have high payoffs. These actions should also include measures to reward regional governments that made progress in establishing the inventory of state-owned property. Similarly, great benefits can be gained from encouraging the design of land use planning tools at the provincial level, including specific criteria and provisions in provincial plans to streamline district-level government decision making on land use within their respective jurisdictions.

Sustainability of Land Policy Achievements

Sustainability of policy changes may involve reducing transaction costs, standardizing assessment by registrars, and designing strategies to encourage property registration. The standardization of registration forms and the elimination of registry control over property and transfer taxes were very effective strategies in the late 1980s, although they have been partly reversed since then. Their reactivation should be combined with awareness campaigns and itinerant registration services, at least in recently formalized settlements. In this context, it will also be necessary to provide a new momentum for the national cadastral system created in 2004 and to establish stronger links between the national cadastral system and the property registry.[26]

KYRGYZ REPUBLIC

The Kyrgyz Republic represents land governance issues arising in a post-transition economy; in fact, it was one of the first countries in the Commonwealth of Independent States to introduce private land ownership when it became independent in 1991. However, large sections of land continue to be owned by the state, and they often are not used effectively. Low population density also suggests that, in many cases, individual titling may not be appropriate. The country is slowly moving toward recognition of communal land rights, which were prevalent before Russian colonization in the late 19th century. The country also implemented a large foreign-funded project to improve land administration.

The transition process from Soviet rule involved major land reforms, beginning with restructuring of some 600 collective farms and liquidation of state landholdings. Given the country's predominantly rural nature and the predominance of agriculture, transfer of arable agricultural land into private ownership was a key step in the social and economic transformation. Introduction of private land ownership was phased in first with the introduction of long-term use rights, then indefinite-term use rights, which were finally converted to ownership, and public land was provided to other entities. Initial stages of privatization involved award of notional land shares to members of collective and state farms without physical identification of plots. Conversion into actual land parcels was undertaken only when a member withdrew from the collective to begin independent farming, a process that was accompanied by issuance of formal documentation of land ownership. Even then, many land titles had either no or highly inaccurate sketches to describe the location of the land. Also, with mass emigration from rural areas, informal and unrecorded sales were frequent. Most of these shortcomings of the transition were addressed by a systematic land registration project supported by the World Bank.

At the same time, state land was not completely transferred. In rural areas, 25 percent of arable agricultural land was left in state ownership to establish a temporary land reserve that was to be used to deal with land claims arising in the transition and in future settlement expansion. This reserve land is now held in a Land Redistribution Fund (LRF) managed by local governments, which offer short-term leases on the land in a process that is often seen as not fully transparent and as failing to provide much-needed government revenues, incentives for investment, or optimum use of the corresponding land. The different tenure situations in the Kyrgyz Republic are presented in table 4.2.

Recognition and Enforcement of Rights

Use rights to individual parcels are guaranteed by law, and a low-cost and far-reaching process of systematic and sporadic titling has by now covered some 92 percent of the country's land parcels. This legal process is complemented by a clear and practical process for formal recognition of long-term unchallenged possession that is implemented effectively, consistently, and transparently, with the possibility of relying on nondocumentary forms of evidence where needed.[27] Moreover, several laws aim to ensure the protection of women's land rights.[28] Though the registry does not identify right holders' gender, studies suggest that some 35 percent to 45 percent of land registered to physical persons is in the name of women. Women's land ownership is higher in regions with active land markets than in remote rural areas, where registration of female rights may clash with customary norms that may preclude them from inheriting land or retaining it in case of divorce. The Kyrgyz Republic also has laws that recognize condominium property and make appropriate arrangements for the management of common property.

Although much land is individually owned, the state remains the Kyrgyz Republic's biggest land owner, and state land is often underused or not managed effectively. With a total of 9 million ha, or 85 percent of the 11 million ha of agricultural land, pastures are the largest land use category in the country. In the past, although de jure rights to such land had to be allocated through competitive leases, pastures near villages remained in common use, and only distant pastures were leased. Nontransparent processes to award leases led to negative equity consequences whereby the best pasture land was often leased by big farmers or well-connected businessmen who then entered into subleases with locals. As a result, the majority of small livestock holders had no access to

Table 4.2 Tenure Typology for the Kyrgyz Republic

Tenure type	Area and population	Legal recognition and characteristics	Overlaps and potential issues
Urban sector			
State land	Private lands Area: 22,514 ha Population: 347,497 owners and users State lands Area: 89,609 ha Population: 11,585 users Municipal lands Area: 21,136 ha Population: 3,445 owners and users	Legal recognition: Ownership rights to private land in municipal areas are recognized subject to registration. Registration/recording: Recorded Transferability: Yes	Can overlap with municipal land if there are no clear boundaries; cases of informal use. Survey (inventory), mapping, and formalization process under way. Coverage thus far is 93% on private property; 72% on state property; and 78% on municipal property.
Private ownership of groups under registered condominiums (RCs)	Extent Bishkek: 219 RCs Osh: 52 RCs Karakol: 7 RCs Population: Unknown	Legal recognition: Condominiums registered as legal entity; right to adjacent land recognized subject to registration Registration/recording: Recorded Transferability: Yes, subject to condominium bylaws	A 2009 regulation limits rights of condominium coowners, specifying that front and back side land areas cannot be owned by the condominium.
Private individual ownership	Area: 22,000 ha Population: 347,000 owners and users Total population: 1.4 million	Legal recognition: Ownership rights to private land in municipal areas recognized subject to registration Registration/recording: Recorded Transferability: Yes	Private ownership can overlap with state and municipal land if no clear boundaries are marked. Transfers in newly settled parts of big towns and cities are often not formalized to avoid cost of registration.

Private individual use of urban land	No data available	Legal recognition: Formalized through contract, which is often not registered (required if longer than 3 years) Registration/recording: Rarely recorded in practice Transferability: Sublease possible if recorded	Many entrepreneurs in urban areas sign lease contracts on municipal land for commerce but do not register those contracts in the state registry.
Private use of common use urban land (informal)	No data available	Legal recognition: Considered to be illegal Registration/recording: Not recorded Transferability: No	Many land plots occupied illegally are recognized by the municipality to avoid social problems.
Rural sector			
State land	Area: 18.6 million ha Population: 40,431 owners and users	Legal recognition: Subject to registration Registration/recording: Recorded Transferability: Yes	The process of surveying, mapping, and formalizing through systematic registration is under way.
Municipal lands	Area: 37,624 ha Population: 5,129 owners and users	Legal recognition: Subject to registration if greater than 3 years Registration/recording: Recorded Transferability: Yes	The process of surveying (inventory), mapping, and formalizing is under way.
Group ownership of rural land	Area: 91,200 ha Population: 77,589	Recognition: Group ownership recognized subject to registration. Registration/recording: Recorded Transferability: Yes	Usually no overlap with other rights is seen.
Communal use of rural land	Area: 3 million ha Population: 1 million	Legal recognition: Not recognized without contract Registration/recording: Not recorded Transferability: No	Communal pasture use is near village pasture and sometimes overlaps with private land. Use can be formalized under the 2009 Pasture Law (February 2009).

(continued next page)

Table 4.2 (Continued)

Tenure type	Area and population	Legal recognition and characteristics	Overlaps and potential issues
Private individual ownership of rural land	Area: 1.06 million ha Population: 905,991	Recognition: Subject to registration Registration/recording: Recorded Transferability: Yes	Private property is protected by the constitution of the Kyrgyz Republic and can be taken only by court decision.
Private individual use of rural land	Area: 1.1 million ha Population: Not available	Legal recognition: Recognized if lease agreements with municipal bodies exist Registration/recording: Recorded Transfer: Sublease allowed for private, not for public or LRF land	Overlap can occur with the state and municipal lands. Land ownership is formalized through contract agreement, but leases often are not registered.
Private use of common-use rural land (informal)	Area: Not available Population: Not available	Legal recognition: Not recognized Registration/recording: Not recorded Transferability: No	Use can include fencing or cultivation of state pastures or unused LRF lands because of land pressure. Rights could be formalized.

Source: Various sources; compiled by A. Undeland.
Note: ha = hectare; LRF = Land Redistribution Fund; RC = registered condominium.

good-quality pastures, prompting them to graze their animals on the communal areas in the immediate proximity of villages and leading to a dramatic degradation of this type of land. To stop this trend, and in the context of overall decentralization, the 2009 Pasture Law replaces leases with the recognition of traditional use rights to pastures and allows these to be registered at the village level, with the responsibility decentralized to pasture users' associations. By transforming leases into use rights that allow seasonal mobility and retention of revenues from pastures at the village level, this law is expected to be an important step in fostering decentralization and more sustainable use of natural resources. Implementing regulations are being drafted.

Policy and Institutional Framework

Policy explicitly accounts for equity goals, with the land code stipulating that every citizen has a right to receive a kitchen or housing plot free once in a lifetime. This had unintended consequences by contributing to large-scale squatting and internal migration, including big waves of squatting in 1989, 1998, and 2005. It also created pressure for the discretionary application of formalization processes on public land.

Forestland (2.7 million ha in total) remains under state ownership and is managed at the national level by the state agency for forestry and environmental protection and at the local level by forestry enterprises. Before being transferred to the national government in 1996, forests were used and managed by collective and state farms. The Forestry Code allows farmers to obtain long-term leases (up to 50 years) on forestland, which includes a vast area of rangeland leased from forestry enterprises by farmers for grazing purposes (*leskhozes*), with revenue going to the agency for forestry and environmental protection, while other pasture land is managed by village governments and pasture user associations with revenue retained at the local level. The different procedures for obtaining use rights to pastures from the Forest Land Fund and from the State Land Fund have led to confusion on the ground and corruption in forestry enterprises.

In rural areas, legal restrictions prevent nonvillagers, foreigners, and legal entities (except those engaged in agricultural production or processing) from purchasing land. Ownership of agricultural land may be transferred only to residents of the same rural area and not to legal entities such as banks or foreigners. Land in settlements may be owned only by Kyrgyz natural persons or by legal entities with majority Kyrgyz ownership. The minimum size of a holding is the share size established in each village during land privatization. The inability of banks to own agricultural land and the fact that any land held by them must be disposed of within a year to avoid the threat of a government buy-out is a disincentive to using land as collateral.

Major strides have been made in the decentralization process to give greater responsibility to elected bodies at the local level and to build up their capacity.

The agencies responsible for managing land and enforcing restrictions are clearly identified and efficient. As a result, land set aside for specific uses is largely used for the intended purpose. Functional distribution of institutional responsibilities (agriculture, environment, and urban use) is reasonably clear, with the possible exception of forest pastures. To increase transparency, the government annually approves and formally publishes a report on the implementation of land policy.[29] Institutions dealing with land management are appropriately staffed and funded, with limited resources to fulfill the mandates of institutions for the management of public land.

Land Use Planning and Taxation

In light of significant urbanization and in-migration, failure to allocate any land to new individual housing in the main cities (including Bishkek) has led to serious shortcomings in housing supply and to dissatisfaction. Town plans are often severely outdated. The main document for town planning is the city's general plan, which, in most cases, dates back to Soviet times, is based on outdated specifications and is out of touch with current realities. Although participation by the public is legally required, such rules are largely ignored in practice, leading to top-down processes of planning and changes of land use that in turn are a major source of conflict and dissatisfaction. Information is often not available publicly, such as changes to land use, modifications to the general city plan, or detailed layout designs and other architectural and town-planning documents that regulate land use. A project to establish town-planning maps and zoning regulations was partly successful; urban land use plans are only partially implemented, and the planning process and planning authority are struggling to cope with the increasing demand for housing units and land.[30]

Land tax rates are very low and vary depending on land use categories,[31] but a failure to account for market values makes the process arbitrary and nontransparent while constraining the potential to raise revenue. Local governments can vary rates within very narrow limits, in addition to carrying out inflation adjustments, but often fail to do so. In a process that gave rise to considerable debate, the land tax was complemented by a property tax that became effective in 2010. Although coverage with land tax is reasonably high, low rates and their infrequent adjustment limit land tax revenue. Especially in urban areas, the rate of tax collection is high and costs are reasonably low. For example, in Bishkek, close to or even more than 100 percent of planned tax collections were realized in 2007 and 2008 because of good tax administration and inclusion of new construction and residential areas, as well as lessors of municipal lands. In secondary cities and villages, tax collection is lower—the average over the past five years in Karakol and Kichi-Kemin is 72 percent and 63 percent, respectively—pointing to considerable potential for higher local revenue.

Public Land Management

Most observers agree that the 25 percent of total arable land that is vested in the state LRF (299,000 ha) is managed very inefficiently, giving rise to rent seeking and corruption on a large scale, and making the LRF one of the major sources of corruption and lost revenue opportunities in the country. No official data are available on the use of the LRF for 2008–09, but the most recent figures, from 2005, show that only slightly more than half of the LRF was leased out. Corruption is widespread—in particular through underreporting of lease rates, nontransparency in land management, lease agreements in the name of third parties who qualify for preferential treatment, and creation of fictitious enterprises that qualify for preferential treatment in allocation of LRF land. By law, the maximum duration of leases for LRF land is 10 years, but in most cases, leases are much shorter, with no clear procedure for renewal, thus undermining incentives for long-term improvements. Under the law, LRF land should be allocated through auction, with priority of land access to be given to women, the poor, and other disadvantaged groups. In practice, unclear rules for auctions and lack of transparency and local involvement have led to allocation of the best lands to local elites.

Expropriation is limited and confined to public uses, with very few cases of expropriated land having been transferred to private uses (two to three cases for the entire country). The Land Code also provides for the purchase of land for public needs, requiring written agreement between the authorized state body and the land user or owner. Appeals processes are available if any of the parties are dissatisfied. Compensation must include the market price for land and structures and any losses to the owner from the termination of rights. The owner has the option of requesting the allocation of a new parcel of land of equal or higher value. At the same time, only registered rights are eligible for compensation, implying that informal rights (for example, for grazing) will not be compensated.

The Land Code requires use of public auctions for disposition of public land but contains a provision that allows land to be given for free without competitive process that is frequently misused. As a result, although the majority of urban land plots are distributed through auctions, most leases of use rights for pastures and some of the leases for LRF land were allocated without an auction process. Local registry data show that the 2008 rental income from the LRF and pasture leases was 87.6 million soms and 13.3 million soms, respectively (US$2.20 million and US$0.33 million, respectively), or some 68 percent and 70 percent of projected revenue, respectively. A key gap, and possible area for policy action, is that despite the recording of the location of public lands and the conditions under which the lands are leased, the information is not publicly available and, in practice, is almost impossible to obtain.[32]

Public Provision of Land Information

A cost-effective process for first-time registration of individual rights has been implemented successfully, suggesting that more than 92 percent of land parcels are registered and that plans to achieve full coverage are under way. Relevant private encumbrances are included in the records, and more than 90 percent of registry records are mapped. Though access to records is limited to intermediaries with demonstrated interest, there are few limits on the number of searches that intermediaries can undertake other than the need to demonstrate an interest and the obligation to pay the necessary fee. Independent surveys have shown that updating of the registry is satisfactory, fee schedules and meaningful service standards are published, receipts are used to discourage informal payments, and the registry operates in a sustainable and self-financing manner with reasonably high levels of customer satisfaction as verified through independent surveys. In addition, the capacity of headquarters and local staff to communicate with clients and other stakeholders has grown significantly since 2009, as a result of public relations training and numerous measures to promote information dissemination and transparency.[33]

Information on individual land is available within the registry; however, that does not mean that all information has been publicly available. In particular, municipal land is defined residually as all land within settlement area borders that is not in private or state ownership and is therefore difficult to identify. Thus, no inventory of municipal land is available, making it impossible to monitor how effectively this valuable resource is being used.[34] Also, although the quality and coverage of land information has greatly improved, huge potential benefits from sharing are forgone because of very weak coordination among relevant institutions and the failure to make full use of the information for strategic decision making.

Documents attesting a transaction must be submitted for registration within 30 days, and unregistered transactions are considered invalid. Although registration is very affordable,[35] fee collections in Kyrgyz registries exceed the operating cost, suggesting that all registration offices are self-financing. Price lists and service standards for operation of all registration services are publicly displayed in each of the offices. Each action is supported by proper receipts and other documents. Boxes to register complaints are available in each of the offices to provide users with an option to register complaints about improper behavior by employees (for example, exacting of informal payments). Access to these boxes is limited to high-level staff members outside the agency. Though insufficient on their own, if complemented by internal vigilance mechanisms, such boxes could help to address the challenge of corruption, which is an issue, especially in areas where property values are high. Capital investments have been covered by an external loan, and a big source of income is systematic registration. The fact that there is no distribution of revenue among registries may suggest that in areas with low levels of real estate market activity, offices will have to either close or merge with each other.[36]

Dispute Resolution and Conflict Management

The Kyrgyz constitution provides for the possibility to establish a court of elders (*aksakal court*) that can make decisions regarding property conflicts within families in each village. These courts are accessible, and their decisions are implemented through peer pressure. Although recent changes that allow participation by women may make the courts more representative, the courts are not always independent or fully representative, and the extent to which their verdicts are recognized by the formal system varies. Clear assignment of responsibilities limits forum shopping, and aggrieved parties can apply to the *rayon* (local government) or city court to have the *aksakal court* decision enforced.

With development of land markets and housing construction, land conflicts are on the increase. Private conflicts regarding the location of borders, over-lapping claims to the same plot, and privatization of land plots by owners of buildings located on them make up some 10 to 30 percent of total court cases. Unresolved cases older than five years represent roughly 5 to 10 percent of total pending court cases. Also, with a rather well-functioning and accessible system for resolving disputes among individuals, many disputes concern conflicts with the state regarding provision of land plots and their withdrawal. Mechanisms to appeal against land-related rulings are available, but associated court fees are very high, taking 10 percent of damages.

Policy Recommendations

Policy recommendations for the Kyrgyz Republic focus on reforming current practices of land redistribution, finding ways to generate more local government revenues from land, and ensuring that information is shared throughout the different institutions involved in the land sector.

Rethinking Land Redistribution

Policies stipulating the right of each citizen to a residential land plot, though seemingly attractive from an equity perspective, are difficult to apply because land is not available. As a result, the policies encourage squatting and will therefore need to be rethought. Similarly, because the reasons that led to the LRF's formation no longer appear to apply, it may be time to rethink the size and justification for the LRF. The situation is even more urgent, because the state appears to be unable to manage the land in question efficiently, suggesting that the country scores poorly on transparency and competition in the disposition of public land.

Although broad distribution of land to the population played an important role in the post-transition economy, the small size of individual land plots has limited the income that can be generated from such plots. As the economy develops, land markets will assume an increasingly important role, and eliminating obstacles to their efficient functioning will be important. Pasture management will need to be improved on the basis of the recent law that decentralizes responsibility to pasture user associations and allows registration of use rights.

Improving Local Government Revenues from Land

With decentralization, the ability to derive revenue from land assumes increasing importance for the supply of local public goods. However, local governments' ability to set land tax rates remains limited. Together with improved tax administration and better definition of municipal lands, this ability could provide local governments with greater autonomy, which could help to establish transparent and participatory processes. These processes will contribute to building local capacity for land use planning and public land management to replace the rigid land use regimes that are no longer in line with reality but continue to provide opportunities for rent-seeking and to decrease land values. Effective local land management will also require closing the loopholes that allow the disposal of public land for free without auction.

Information Sharing

The Kyrgyzstan land administration project includes many best practice elements that can provide lessons. Barriers to information sharing among different government agencies dealing with land are gradually being overcome, including the development of ways to register lands that are not held individually and to make sure that such information is publicly available. All the information regarding real estate and land over the country that exists in local registration offices has been merged in a Kyrgyz Land Information System. Plans exist to make such information publicly available online, with provisions to sell bulk data at set fees.

TANZANIA

Tanzania has spent considerable amounts of time and effort to develop a land policy in a participatory way.[37] However, although the government adopted an ambitious agenda to formalize property (known locally as MKURABITA), implementation of the 1999 Land Act (LA) and Village Land Act (VLA), which aims to make this policy operational, has advanced little since the legislation was adopted. A closer look at this case study can offer lessons for African countries that exhibit a similar pattern of ambitious legal change followed by limited implementation on the ground.

Rights Recognition

Land in mainland Tanzania falls into one of three types: village land, reserved land, or general land (table 4.3). Village land, which covers about

Table 4.3   Tenure Typology for Tanzania

Tenure type	Area and population	Legal recognition and characteristics	Issues and potential overlaps
Urban sector			
Private individual use of urban land, formal (right of occupancy, for which a certificate is issued for 33, 66, or 99 years)	Area: 10,400 ha Population: 1.6 million Number: 350,000 titles Number of open letters of offer: Unknown	Legal recognition: Recognized if development conditions are met and land rent is paid; eligible for compensation if expropriated Registration: Rights recorded (Registration starts by issuing a letter of offer for a right of occupancy; acceptance triggers issuance of a certificate of right of occupancy [CRO].) Transferability: Transferable with consent by the commissioner	The following issues are noted: Double allocations that lead to dispute, lack of service infrastructure, slow development of land after allocation, nonconformity with development conditions, long period to issue title or to transfer.
Private individual use of urban land, semiformal (a derivative right with duration of 2–5 years [renewable], known as residential license [RL].)	Area: 680 ha Population: 1.6 million owners Properties surveyed: 263,000 Applied for RL: 91,000 RLs issued: 86,000	Legal recognition: Recognized under Section 23 of 1999 Land Act (LA) Registration/recording: Recorded as a result of a survey by the Ministry of Lands, Housing, and Human Settlement Development Boundaries: Not definite, subject to regularization Transferability: Yes, subject to subdivision restrictions	Demand and renewal rates are limited. Collateral has limited usefulness. No process exists for upgrading RL to CRO.

(continued next page)

Table 4.3 (Continued)

Tenure type	Area and population	Legal recognition and characteristics	Issues and potential overlaps
Private individual use of urban land, informal (land obtained informally with no or limited involvement of public authorities)	Area: 51,350 ha Population: 6.4 million	Legal recognition: Tenure undefined; owners can be considered "deemed licensees" as per section 23 of LA; taxes paid, compensation for expropriation; access to services Registration/recording: Not recorded Transferability: Informal transfers only (no planning norms)	Extension of urban boundaries into village land creates uncertainty over tenure in such areas unless village land is converted into general land. Conflicts are frequent when land is acquired for planned urban development.
Communal use of urban land (group/condominium type of use or tenure)	Area: Negligible Population: Negligible	Legal recognition: Recognized under 2007 Unit Titles Act and Land Act; s.t. adherence to development conditions Registration: Registry of condominiums to be established Transferability: Yes, s.t. restrictions by condominium association	Unit Titles Act is new and has yet to be used to any significance, but condominium use of urban property is likely to grow in the future.
Informal occupation of state urban land (legal squatting)	Area: 2,600 ha Population: 400,000	Legal recognition: Tenure undefined (owners can be considered deemed licensees per section 23 of LA. Registration: Recorded only in exceptional circumstances Transferability: Informal transfers only	Land could be encroached upon if not clearly demarcated and looked after. Privatization of public land raised concerns, especially if not done at market prices.

Rural sector			
General land			
Private individual use of rural land	Area: 1.1 million ha Population: 200,000	Legal recognition: Right of occupancy up to 99 years by large-scale farmers or investors; recognized under 1999 LA; foreign investors' land vested in tenancy in common or a joint venture Registration: Yes Transferability: Yes, subject to consent by commissioner of lands	One concern is that current or potential village land will be passed to investors to the detriment of villagers. A second concern is about wide powers held by the commissioner of lands to convert village land to general land without adequate consultation.
Village land			
Private individual land use under Certificate of Customary Right of Occupancy (CCRO) (customary individual tenure; indefinite duration; no development conditions)	Area: 4.1 million ha Population: 26 million	Legal recognition: Recognized under Village Land Act 1999. Registration: Hardly any CCROs issued (issuance is contingent on survey of village boundaries and issuance of a certificate of village land [CVL]) Transferability: Unrestricted within village; difficult outside	Recognition overlaps with general land in peri-urban areas. CVL must be issued to allow issuance of CCROs.

(*continued next page*)

Table 4.3 (Continued)

Tenure type	Area and population	Legal recognition and characteristics	Issues and potential overlaps
Communal use of rural land; customary communal tenure	Area: 35 million ha Population: 3 million	Legal recognition: Recognized under 1999 VLA Registration: Not recorded except for a few villages with land use plans Boundaries: No demarcation Transferability: No	Overlaps with individual villages and reserved land (parks, game reserves, conservation areas) are unclear. Many disputes between pastoralists and farmers occur. Pastoralists are frequently removed from "their" land.
Reserved land Informal occupation of reserved land (legal squatting)	Area: 7.6 million ha Population: 300,000 to 1 million	Legal recognition: Much not surveyed and not titled Registration/recording: Recorded (gazetted) Transferability: No	Reserved land overlaps with pastoral lands, village lands, and state lands. Conflicts occur with farmers and pastoralists.

Source: Various sources; compiled by L. Kironde.

Note: CCRO = certificate of customary right of occupancy; CRO = certificate of right of occupancy; CVL = certificate of village land; ha = hectare; LA = Land Act (1999); RL = residential license; s.t. = strata title (condominium); VLA = Village Land Act (1999).

70 percent of mainland Tanzania and accommodates 28 million to 30 million people, is under the jurisdiction and management of registered villages. Reserved land, which covers 28 percent of the mainland, comprises forest-land, conservation areas, national parks, and game reserves. General land, about 2 percent of the mainland area, consists of all land that is neither village land nor reserved land.

Because Tanzania consists of a vast countryside with only a few urban areas, most land in the country is village land, that is, land under the jurisdiction and management of a registered village according to the 1999 VLA.[38] To adhere to the provisions of the VLA, the village first must acquire a certificate of village land. The certification procedure requires agreement on the perimeter borders among neighboring villages. Once consensus is reached and the border is prop-erly demarcated and surveyed, a formal certificate of village land is issued in the name of the President and is registered in the National Register of Village Land. However, because not all villages are registered, the legal status of land in unregistered villages is unclear. Registered villages are required to define three land use categories within their borders: (a) communal village land, (b) individual and family land, and (c) reserved land. Reserved land in this context is to be understood as land set aside for future individual or commu-nal use and needs to be distinguished from the national category of reserved land. National reserved land includes land reserved as forests, conservation areas, national parks, and game reserves. It amounts to some 28 percent of mainland Tanzania and is not supposed to be occupied, although it is esti-mated that about 300,000 to 1 million people informally occupy reserved land. General land consists of all land that is neither village land nor reserved land. All land in urban areas, with an estimated population of some 10 mil-lion, falls under this type, except areas that are covered by laws constituting reserved land or that are considered hazardous land. General land is governed by the LA and, hence, is under the control and jurisdiction of the President, as represented by the Commissioner of Lands, who also can convert village land into general land.

Each of these categories presents some challenges. Issuance of the certifi-cate of village land would then allow issuance of certificates of customary right of occupancy to individual landholders within the village sporadically on a demand-driven basis. However in early 2010, more than a decade after passage of the relevant legislation, only 753 of Tanzania's 10,397 registered villages (or 7 percent) had received certificates, which raises concerns mainly because of the lack of clarity about the legal status of land in unregistered villages.[39] The status of "squatters" (estimated to number between 300,000 and 1 million) on national reserved land is also unclear. Though the rights of those who took possession in good faith are protected by law, cut-off dates were not clarified. Informal rights in urban tenure, even if not recorded, enjoy protection against eviction and are eligible for compensation, and nondocu-mentary evidence is accepted.

Policy and Institutional Framework

Although Tanzania's land policy has been developed in a participatory process, progress with implementation has been minimal. Examination of the system illustrates a number of reasons for this. First, strong security of land rights of settled populations does not extend to the marginalized. Pastoralists or shifting cultivators who have not received any group tenure certificates often have their rights infringed upon in the context of land use planning. The legislation also makes little effort to establish more progressive patterns of female land ownership, suggesting that women's land rights and inheritance follow traditional or customary patterns. Second, whereas tenure security for most land users (even those occupying land informally) is considered to be high, transferability is limited by restrictions on village lands that cannot be changed at a decentralized level and by a highly centralized, cumbersome, and high-cost approval process by the Commissioner of Lands that adds little value but can create enormous bottlenecks.[40] Third, the incentives for ending informality are weak; formalization processes are complex and often high cost, so most occupants, even in high-income urban areas, remain in informality. For example, 80 percent of housing in the major city of Dar es Salaam (400,000 out of 500,000 houses) remains informal. High fees and unrealistic planning standards make formalization very difficult and out of the reach of the poor. In addition, a policy that insists on full cost recovery points toward gaps in the institutional structure. As a result, even recent high-profile efforts to increase formality have not had the desired success. More than two-thirds (68 percent) of urban developments have been carried out without valid permits and in contravention of approved plans, something that has a negative effect on the ability to use land as collateral. Moreover, the poor are entirely shut out of the formal system. Even registered village lands can easily be incorporated into urban expansion through processes that involve minimal compensation, suggesting that benefits from obtaining village certificates are not obvious. It is therefore not surprising that progress in formalizing these village lands remains slow as well.

Land Use Planning and Taxation

The fact that urban land settlement expands rapidly into very rural areas without any subsequent urbanization creates tenure insecurity for villagers. This situation, together with an inability to bring the land to the destined use or to even demarcate public areas, such as road reserves, encourages informal occupation, thus contributing to squatting and uncontrolled urban expansion. For example, land earmarked for schools or markets may remain undemarcated or undeveloped for years, thus encouraging invasion. This uncontrolled expansion is further encouraged by the lack of access to information about what is public land. Unrealistic building standards further exacerbate this situation. Although minimum plot sizes are set at 400 square meters, survey evidence shows that almost 87.5 percent of urban residents live on plots that measure less than this amount, thus forcing the majority into informality. However, rather than making plot sizes more realistic, the government revised plot size restrictions upward in 1997, and a debate about making them even larger is currently under way.

Although property tax can, in principle, be the backbone of local government finance and effective decentralization, Tanzania's complex, costly, and nontransparent valuation processes make updating of valuation rolls difficult and result in assessed values quickly becoming out of date. This situation deprives local authorities of much-needed revenue; current collection is estimated to yield only 30 percent of potential. Because most property tax revenue must be transferred to the central government, local governments' incentives for more effective collection are weak. Recent efforts to transfer property tax collection to the Tanzania Revenue Authority did not address this issue and, indeed, were unsuccessful because of a lack of capacity.

Public Land Management

In most cases, the types of land assigned to public land ownership are justified by the desire to provide public goods; however, responsibility for managing these lands in many cases either is not clearly assigned between local authorities, sector ministries, and public agencies or is at a level inconsistent with effective and efficient public administration. Moreover, an inventory of public lands and their geographical location does not exist and normally is undertaken only on an ad hoc basis, such as if divestiture is contemplated. No information about availability of public lands is accessible to the public. This lack of information not only encourages informal occupation of public land by squatters, but also makes it very difficult to assess the efficiency of the public institutions that manage such lands. Detecting and acting to reduce inefficiencies are therefore difficult, an issue that is important, because in many cases, responsibility to manage public land may be with authorities or agencies that lack the necessary capacity. Investors are unable to get a good sense of land availability without incurring major transaction costs, something that recently prompted the government to establish a bank of land that has been cleared preemptively from all interest to make it available for investors.

Expropriation is a major problem for a number of reasons. First, it is routinely used to acquire land for subsequent transfer to private interests in the name of either rational town planning or productive rural investment.[41] Virtually all the land for urban expansion or establishment of large-scale private investment (for mining, farming, or hunting) in rural areas is obtained through expropriation. The regressive nature of this policy, which is perceived as aiming to push out poor and indigenous landowners to allow the rich or the state to derive major benefits, has led to strong criticism. Other options to attain the desired objective may need to be explored.

Second, the process is seen as arbitrary, and avenues for appeal are ill-defined and weak. Reports of cases where buildings were demolished even while appeals were pending, or where expropriated owners were, after long delays, asked to either "take or leave" the compensation on offer after their land had been taken, do little to strengthen confidence in the fairness of the process or the ability of land users to uphold existing rights. Third, formulas to determine compensation are unclear and are viewed as being applied arbitrarily and inconsistently. With public authorities using their powers arbitrarily to determine payment values and, in some cases, collaborating openly with and acting on behalf of future land users, transparency or independence in the way compensation is determined is perceived to be limited. Lack of transparency also applies to the disposition of expropriated land through subsequent transactions. The fact that these negotiations are not conducted openly and that agreements with the buyer or lessee are not publicly accessible limits the scope for effective enforcement, causes mistrust, and undermines security of property rights through fear of future expropriation.

Public Provision of Land Information

As the tenure typology illustrated, at most 7 percent of land plots in the country are registered, though the number of letters of offer issued is not known even to land institutions. Out of these, less than 50 percent can be identified on maps, and less than 70 percent of records are estimated to be up-to-date. At present, the registry is starved of capital investment and cannot sustain itself from the fees charged. Instead, it is financed as part of the Ministry of Lands, Housing, and Human Settlements Development, completely eliminating the link between collection of fees and registry activity or income—an issue that needs to be addressed together with decentralization.

Copies or extracts of documents recording rights in property can be obtained by paying stipulated fees, a schedule that is publicly available. Receipts are issued for all transactions. However, despite steps to computerize the process, most searches are still done manually. A client service charter has been established, but service standards seem arbitrary and, in some cases, technically impossible, suggesting that little serious effort has gone into the charter and little enforcement or follow-up is done. In line with this conclusion, levels of customer satisfaction are not monitored or used as a management tool.

Dispute Resolution and Conflict Management

In an effort to make judicial services more accessible, a 2002 law established a new structure of land courts with four tiers (village councils, ward land and housing tribunals, district land and housing tribunals, and a land division of the High Court). However, instead of improving access to justice, the system resulted in an increased number of conflicts and the accumulation of a backlog of unresolved cases. A main reason for the delays was that, instead of using informal dispute resolution to resolve issues quickly, lower-level courts adopted court-like proceedings. Thus, although a multiplicity of institutions are available for lodging applications to resolve private conflicts, there is very limited scope for dealing with intercommunity conflicts or conflicts between individuals and the state.

Furthermore, overlaps in jurisdiction—from the fact that ward councils are administered by local authorities; district tribunals are administered by the Ministry of Lands, Housing, and Human Settlements Development; and the High Court is administered by the Ministry of Justice and Constitutional Affairs—have led to widespread forum shopping, possibly even making access to justice more unequal as a result of the reform. Establishing a coherent structure would thus be of great importance. The rather unsatisfactory performance of the justice system is illustrated by the fact that less than half the land-related conflicts are resolved in the first-instance court within one year, and more than 20 percent of the total pending land dispute cases have been in court for more than five years.

Policy Recommendations

Tanzania's land policy, which was adopted in 1996 and formalized in the new land laws of 1999, is now more than 10 years old, and it seems fair to say that the policy has not lived up to expectations. A systematic review to explore the extent to which expected gains have materialized and what can be done to improve performance of the land sector would be highly desirable. Some of the issues that are likely to be touched upon by such a review are highlighted as follows, including efforts for surveys, mapping, and registration; affirmative action to address gender issues; the redefinition of institutional mandates; the strengthening of decentralization; more participatory land use planning; changes in expropriation practices; and ways to improve conflict resolution mechanisms.

Surveys, Mapping, and Registration

Absence of maps and land records is a key reason that Tanzania's well-designed and rather elaborate land system is ineffective at securing users' rights. Mapping and low-cost registration of land at the communal level (for village land) or individual level (for urban land) can help defend land rights against challengers and help foster markets. The effort should be linked to land use planning in a way that ensures documentation and preservation of secondary and pastoral rights. To facilitate this, the government will need to establish basic infrastructure and update the 1957 Land Surveying Ordinance to allow cost-effective, lower-precision surveys that can be undertaken by private surveyors. Procedures for first-time and subsequent registration need to be reviewed and simplified (for example, by cutting out unnecessary duplication and requiring approval from the appropriate levels) to encourage landowner participation.

Gender

With less than 20 percent of the land registered in the name of women, gender issues need immediate attention. Public education and affirmative action by public authorities is necessary to encourage more women to get land registered in their names or jointly with spouses. Efforts to train and deploy more female land professionals are also recommended.

Institutional Structure

The Ministry of Lands, Housing, and Human Settlements Development will need to perform oversight more effectively, to set broad policy and guidelines, and to monitor developments. The land registry, as well as any potential approvals, should be decentralized and provide integrated services for all village and general land, rather than having two registries. The ministry should spearhead development of land information systems and encourage information sharing between authorities dealing with land and land resources. It should also monitor the effect of its own activities more rigorously with the goal of identifying good practice that can be scaled up by other agents. The requirement that any land transfer be signed by the Commissioner of Lands in the capital has developed into a tremendous roadblock to the functioning of land markets. It adds little, if any, value and is likely to distract the ministry from more important tasks.

Decentralization

As part of the ongoing local government reform, and in line with the government policy of decentralization, local authorities need to be allowed to assume greater responsibilities in the land area.[42] But it will also be important to strengthen the material, financial, and human capacity of local authorities and ease the way for them to better tap into property tax as a potential source of revenue. An annual budget to update the valuation roll and improve enforcement can go a long way in this direction. Allowing a larger part of property tax revenue to go toward improving local infrastructure and land information services would also establish proper incentives. Both the Ministry of Lands and local authorities should work on modalities of surplus capture, through a property tax or a specific levy, from change of use, issuance of planning permission, or construction of infrastructure. Investment in capital equipment and human capacity is important for enabling the land registry to play a more active role. The highly inadequate current level of resources available to the registry could be increased by charging realistic fees in return for better services. In this context, options for the land registry to become an independent and self-financing agency should be further explored, for both urban and rural land.

Land Use Planning

The National Land Use Planning Commission, which is based on the Rural Development Policy and shares authority with rural authorities, should ensure that all rural land (including that overseen by township authorities) is planned using participatory methods. This approach is needed to recognize and secure the rights of transhumant groups such as pastoralists, hunters, gatherers, and other vulnerable communities, which are widely neglected at this point. The participatory planning approach would also help demarcate reserved land and avoid slum creation in the future. Although there is a rural development policy, no corresponding urban development policy exists. Such a policy, which would cover urban land management and administration, needs to be developed expeditiously. It can provide the basis for participatory establishment of land use plans to guide development of urban areas and townships in a way that would eliminate uncertainty and help guide the behavior of those interested in acquiring land or migrating from other areas. Both communities and the private sector should then be allowed to plan and survey land in accordance with public authorities' plans as a precondition for allowing urban areas to cope with growth. An immediate next step is to reformulate plot standards to increase density of use. Such a step would benefit the urban poor, who would be able to afford such plots, as well as public authorities, who would be able to service such land at lower unit cost.

Expropriation

Expropriation is quickly emerging as a major source of clashes between public authorities and landowners. The proposed review of the Land Acquisition Act 1967 should be fast-tracked and undertaken with extensive public exposure and debate while building on best practice internationally and leaving expropriation as a last resort after attempts at reaching negotiated settlements have failed. Even then, expropriation proceedings—as well as those involving divestiture of any state assets—need to be conducted in a much more transparent manner. Independent valuation of land assets should be the norm and should replace the current practice of having government assess the value of the assets it acquires, which creates serious conflicts of interest. Eligibility for compensation should not be limited to owners but also be made available to tenants and dependents (that is, spouses and children). Contrary to current practice, compensation should also be offered for land use changes if they lead to loss of assets (for example, expansion of urban boundaries that eliminates land rights of rural communities or land use changes that lead pastoralists to lose grazing land or cattle). Ways for those affected to maintain their living standards need to be part of the compensation package. An immediate institution of appeal that can make a quick decision in the case of dissatisfaction of either party will be needed to ensure appropriate incentives.

Disputes

The most promising way to minimize land disputes in the long term will be through (a) consensual identification and recording of boundaries that will improve land information, (b) more accessible and responsive institutions, and (c) greater transparency in procedures involving land transactions. Still, current mechanisms to resolve disputes among individuals are problematic. The government adopted quasi-judicial procedures that are very slow and, as outside the judiciary, lack the capacity for enforcement. Instead, it seems that the majority of existing disputes could easily be solved by alternative dispute resolution mechanisms, which need to be encouraged and their decisions supported by the formal system. Also needed are mechanisms to effectively resolve intercommunity disputes—especially between pastoralists and sedentary farmers, which are becoming increasingly frequent—and to provide individuals wronged by the state with effective ways to seek quick and effective redress.

ETHIOPIA

Ethiopia is not only poor, but also land scarce, with its rain-fed highlands having some of the highest population densities in Africa. Land is of great economic and political relevance, and it is not surprising that major political upheavals over the past four decades have all been accompanied by dramatic shifts in the pattern of land ownership and access.[43] Being a federal state, Ethiopia also has considerable regional autonomy in land laws and land governance.

Recognition and Enforcement of Rights

Ethiopia's legal framework comprises its constitution, federal laws (the civil code, the 1997 rural land law as amended in 2005, and the 1993 urban land law as amended in 2002), and regional laws and directives.[44] These stipulate that all land is owned by the government, but use rights of holdings are recognized: private individual; communal, in rural areas; and condominium, in urban areas (tables 4.4 and 4.5). Some heterogeneity occurs across regions, which are assigned responsibility for land management and administration by the constitution.

In rural areas by 2009, only the four main regions (Amhara; Oromia; Tigray; and the Southern Nations, Nationalities, and Peoples [SNNP]), which account for some 70 percent of the rural population, had passed implementing legislation or regulations to issue land certificates that recognize individual rights.[45] Thus far, registration and certification of rural private holdings have covered 85 percent of rural households in the four regions. Though individual rights are recognized, their transferability is restricted in a number of ways. Private

Table 4.4 Tenure Typology for Ethiopia, Rural Sector

Tenure type	Legal recognition and characteristics
Public land	Legal recognition: Recognized as state holding in the Rural Land Administration and Land Use Proclamation (No. 456/2005) and regional land laws.
	Registration/recording: Although all rural land is to be measured and registered, only four regions undertook relevant programs that focused on individual holdings, thus leaving out a large portion of land. The majority of state forestlands and protected areas are yet to be demarcated and registered.
	Transferability: Public land cannot be transferred, only allocated by the government. Under Article 5 of Proclamation No. 456/2005, the government can allocate rural land to be used by peasants and pastoralists (free of charge), investors, and nongovernmental and other social and economic institutions.
Private individual holding	Legal recognition: The right of rural households to acquire (perpetual) rights to land free of charge is recognized under article 40/4f of the constitution.
	Registration/recording: Four of the nine regional states established systems to record individual rural holdings covering an estimated 70 percent of total population.
	Transferability: Private individual holdings cannot be sold and can be transferred only through inheritance to family members practicing agriculture and living with the right holder. Holdings can be leased to other farmers or investors, subject to restrictions on the extent and duration of leases.
Private communal holding	Legal recognition: Access rights to communal holding over rural land are recognized by the constitution and proclamations (Proc. No. 456/2005).
	Registration/recording: No registration occurs except for pilot cases.
	Transferability: Because they have access rights only, community members cannot transfer rights to common resources. "Government being the owner of rural land, communal rural land holdings can be changed to private holdings as may be necessary" (Proc. No. 456/2005, Art. 5-3).
Commercial holding (investors)	Legal recognition: Private investors can acquire time-bound use rights over rural land to engage in commercial activities through contract with the state (Proc. No. 456/2005, Art. 5-8).
	Registration/recording: Rural land up to 5,000 ha is given to investors by regional investment authorities, with allocations beyond this being made by the federal authority. Overlapping institutional authorities and weak capacity suggest that data are weak.
	Transferability: Investors who hold rural land through lease or rent have the right to transfer and use as collateral their holding right.

Source: Various sources; compiled by I. Tamrat.

Table 4.5 Tenure Typology for Ethiopia, Urban Sector

Tenure type	Legal recognition and characteristics
Public land	Legal recognition: Because the state is the owner of all lands (Articles 40/3 and 40/4 of the constitution), urban lands are managed and controlled by the government through its different agencies. Lands not held by individuals or investors through permits or leases could be considered public land.
	Registration/recording: Recording and registration of urban land is limited and is neither comprehensive nor effective, although figures are difficult to obtain.
	Transferability: Public land can be allocated and transferred to individuals or investors through lease (Urban Land Lease Holding Proc. No. 272/2002).
Private residential (permit)	Legal recognition: Although the leasehold system applies to all urban lands irrespective of how the lands were held previously (Proc. No. 272/2002), the law in effect recognizes residential land acquired by permit until authorities decide on the full application of the leasehold system, which is not the case in most regional states and city governments.
	Registration/recording: There is a limited practice of recording and registering urban land under private holdings, including land held through a permit system by the municipalities of major urban centers. However, the practice lacks comprehensiveness and effectiveness.
	Transferability: The holding right over a private residential holding through a permit system can be transferred through sale, inheritance, or other means. However, transfer through sale or change of use to commercial use results in the conversion of the permit system into leasehold.
Private leasehold	Legal recognition: Proclamation No. 272/2002 provides for lease holding of all new residential land allocation as of 1993 and all urban residential land transferred other than through inheritance as of 1993.
	Registration/recording: Private residential holdings through the leasehold system are registered by the concerned municipalities, although the registration is not systematic and comprehensive.
	Transferability: According to Article 13 of the lease proclamation, any leasehold processor can transfer, or undertake a surety on, right of leasehold and may also use it as a capital contribution to the amount of the lease payment.

Commercial holding (condominium used for residential purposes)	Legal recognition: Under the Condominium Proclamation (No. 370/2003), unit holders of a condominium have rights to use common elements, including the landholding. Registration/recording: Condominium holdings are registered by the concerned municipalities. Transferability: Unit holders of a condominium have a right to sell or transfer their unit, which also results in the transfer of rights on common elements.
Informal residential	Legal recognition: Formalization of informal residential holdings is not addressed in the lease proclamation. Some initiatives to formalize settlements based on directives by local government have been undertaken on the basis of adverse possession rules. Registration/recording: Informal residential holdings are not registered until they are formalized, at which point they cease to be informal holdings. Transferability: Because informal residential holdings are not recognized in the eyes of the law, they cannot be legally transferred.
Commercial holding (condominium used for commercial purposes)	Legal recognition: Proclamation No. 272/2002 provides for lease holding of all urban land used for commercial purposes. However, regional laws apply to both lease and rent arrangements for commercial property in different urban centers within a region. Registration/recording: Urban land holdings for commercial purposes through leasehold or permit systems are registered by the concerned municipalities, although the registration is not systematic and comprehensive. Transferability: According to Article 13 of Proclamation No. 272/2002, any leasehold processor, including a lease holder for commercial purposes, can transfer, or undertake a surety on, right of leasehold and may also use it as a capital contribution to the amount of the lease payment made.

Source: Various sources; compiled by I. Tamrat.

holdings cannot be sold or otherwise transferred except through inheritance, which is restricted to coresident family members, suggesting that mortgages are not possible.[46] Although rents are allowed, in most regions only part of a holding can be rented out, and there are upper limits on the lease period.[47] The constitution maintains that all rural Ethiopians can get use rights to rural land free of charge. To make this feasible, the government can acquire and reallocate land that either is not used or is held by individuals who are not community residents. This may significantly limit tenure security. Subdivision below a minimum parcel size of 0.5 ha in rural areas and 2.0 ha in resettlement areas is also prohibited. Though these restrictions may appear justified from a perspective of equity or productivity, they may in practice contribute little to either or even have perverse effects, may lead to informality, or may hinder rural income diversification.

The laws also are not clear with regard to communal landholdings because they lack provisions about the nature of those rights and of ways to record or enforce them. The resulting legal vacuum threatens to undermine equity and effective management of common property resources. This hazard is particularly relevant for pastoralists (15 percent of the rural population), whose rights, despite a communal use pattern, appear to be treated as individual ones. Without a clear definition, ad hoc practices have often been adopted in land certification, with such lands often registered in the name of the *kebele* (village) government. This practice is not conducive to effective management and may lead to encroachment and poor management of such lands.

In urban areas, the Urban Land Lease Holding Proclamation No. 272/2002 (the Lease Proclamation) stipulates that land is allocated through auctions of permits or sold under a lease system requiring payment to the state. The law does not provide criteria to determine when urban land is to be granted on lease or when it should be allocated through negotiations. This lack of clarity leads to coexistence of the old permit system (permits granted prior to 1993), under which an annual land rent is paid to the government, and the new lease system (from 1993 onward), which requires payment of the agreed-on lease amount to the relevant government within a period of time to be determined by regions or city government within the lease contract. The Lease Proclamation stipulates that the leasehold system will apply to all urban lands irrespective of how they were acquired. However, the fact that the relevant authorities have to first adopt the leasehold system, something that has rarely happened, leaves ample room for discretion.[48] For example, whereas large towns in Amhara have moved to the lease system, smaller towns have adopted a permit-rent system on a virtually permanent basis. Even under the lease system, payment schedules are excessively complicated, and amounts collected total only a fraction of market values, suggesting that local governments lose large amounts of revenue and the system may not be sustainable.

In contrast to practices for rural land, urban leases or permits are fully transferable.[49] However, the lease proclamation fails to deal with formalization of informal residential holdings. Rules of adverse possession (long-term peaceful use without legitimate challenge over a period of 15 years) that are still operational under the civil code may provide some legal basis for recognizing squatters' rights. However, because the code refers to private rights only, its applicability is far from certain. Also, transfer of rights through sale or change of use for commercial purposes will convert the permit into leasehold.

Condominium holdings, which have become widespread in urban areas, are also recognized under Condominium Proclamation No. 370/2003. That document provides clear rules regarding the management of the building, but it lacks clarity regarding the rights to the land beneath the common property. Apart from condominium holdings, there is no legal recognition of communal holdings such as green areas, forestland, playing fields, and so forth in urban areas, although such holdings exist and are identified in urban plans.

Ethiopia's civil code requires all immovable properties to be registered as evidence of ownership. However, the notary public that is anticipated by the code has never been established. Instead, authentication of title documents and recording of transactions in immovable property are undertaken by municipalities and the deeds registration offices that they have established. Such records are the only legally acceptable evidence of rights over immovable property. Registration of individual holdings in urban areas is lagging rural areas; in 2006, the share of registered housing units was estimated to be 95 percent in Adama (Oromia), 65 percent in Addis Ababa (Oromia), 50 percent in Bahirdar (Amhara), 75 percent in Hawassa (SNNP), and 90 percent in Mekelle (Tigray). If one takes into account that a large number of holdings have not yet been formalized, only about 25 percent of the existing individually held urban properties are estimated to be registered in these offices.

Between 35 percent and 45 percent of land registered to physical persons is estimated to be registered in the name of women, with variations across regions. In Amhara, more than 85 percent of certificates name a woman as individual or joint holder, but this share is lower in Oromia and SNNP, where polygamy is more common and holdings are registered in the name of individuals rather than households. Still, there is no doubt that the campaign to register land has significantly improved women's land rights. The requirement in Amhara and Oromia not only to list females' names on certificates but also to have their pictures attached appears to have had a very positive effect in this respect.

Though informal settlements account for up to 30 percent of residential holdings in Addis Ababa, no policies or procedures require the systematic regularization of informal holdings. In fact, formalization projects have no basis in federal legislation, and the few sporadic initiatives to formalize existing settlements (in Addis Ababa, Diredawa, and Hawassa) were very costly and of a discretionary nature. Established by ad hoc municipal directives, they lacked transparency and were discontinued without reaching their targets.

Policy and Institutional Framework

In principle, assignment of responsibilities for policy making and implementation is unambiguous: the federal level formulates policies; regional or municipal governments are responsible for implementation and management of land administration; and the judiciary resolves disputes that might arise in the process. The practice is more complex and could give rise to concerns regarding governance.

Although no single document sets out Ethiopia's land policy, principles can be inferred from federal laws, together with the laws and directives promulgated by regional and municipal governments. However, the wide delegation of federal mandates to lower levels of government, without sufficient policy guidelines or laws to clearly define the roles of various levels of government, causes ambiguities and vertical overlap.[50] In fact, the mandates on land allocation and administration to the different levels of government within a regional state are usually determined by unpublished administrative directives that often change quickly and without public notice. These practices are not in line with principles of good governance. This problem is mirrored on the side of the judiciary, where unclear mandates of federal first-instance courts, municipal courts, and land clearance and appeals commissions create temptations for forum shopping and contradictory rulings.

In addition to unclear responsibilities at different levels of government, horizontal overlap is an issue. In rural areas, both the land administration institutions and the investment authorities have a mandate to allocate land to investors. In Addis Ababa, there is lack of clarity regarding the roles of the central administration and the 10 subcities in allocating land and administering rights over land. In one case, this complexity led to allocation of public use areas to construction of housing and commercial buildings. Although the municipal agency responsible for management of parks and green areas in Addis Ababa belatedly identified the trespass of its mandate, no action was taken, because construction had already begun. The fact that the allocating authority felt secure in its mandate to manage the concerned areas, together with the delayed and ineffective response by the agency that was by law responsible for making decisions, illustrate the extent to which mandates are confused and the effect on land governance.

Some institutions have prerogatives for both policy making and implementation, which may lead to conflicts of interest. Three prominent cases are (a) the Ministry of Agriculture, regarding management of forestland and wildlife; (b) the delegation of legislative powers on important policy issues to regional and municipal land administration authorities, in addition to the authorities' primary policy implementation mandates; and (c) the fact that members of the executive who decide on expropriation may sit with the Clearance Order Appeals Commission that decides appeals in expropriation cases. The widespread practice of assigning members of legislative councils and executive committees to serve on land administration committees and lease boards, which have both executive and adjudicatory functions, can also create conflicts of interest. This possibility is not only theoretical; the fact that these committee members sit concurrently on the respective regional or municipal executive councils is reported to have led to the issuance of directives that were specifically targeted to influence the resolution of specific cases.

In addition to the constitutional provision that gives every rural Ethiopian the right to a plot of land, rural land laws explicitly recognize land rights of orphans and women. The corresponding urban land lease laws have provisions making reference to women and persons who have disabilities or who are physically challenged.[51] However, the equity effect of land policies is not systematically monitored in a way that allows public scrutiny. Although land institutions submit periodic reports, the source and reliability of the underlying data are not always clear. Also, though participatory procedures for lawmaking are enacted and further reinforced by the apparent decentralization of decision making, many laws were developed by experts with little or no public consultation prior to draft laws being forwarded to the legislature. Even in cases of consultation, as in the case of developing the building code, input was by invitation only, something that may exclude many relevant stakeholders such as the academic community and other non–state actors.

Land Use Planning

Except for a recent initiative covering development corridors and areas around Addis Ababa, no master plans are prepared for most rural areas in Ethiopia. In urban areas, the law envisions development guided or controlled by urban plans. Although attempts to establish land use plans have begun in Addis Ababa, most city plans are prepared at a central level, often with little link to reality. Changes to land use plans are rarely publicized in advance of implementation, and virtually no public consultation occurs in the land use planning processes. In Addis Ababa, the involvement of the public in the preparation of a new master plan was limited to an announcement about the status of the process and the publication of the resulting master plan. The involvement of the population in drafting new building height restrictions was nominal. Little notice is given before land use changes: owners of properties affected by a planned road project do not receive any notice before site transfer. Property owners mostly learn of changes in land use covering their properties only when their applications for permits are processed.

City plans do not keep up with actual developments on the ground. In Addis Ababa, where reference points or coordinates used for the city are erroneous and their locations are inaccessible, detailed land use classification is not undertaken, even after the land use changes. Cities struggle with the increased demand for housing that results from city growth, especially in peri-urban areas, but they do little land use planning. In most cases, development moves ahead of planning in an informal way that makes both cost-effective provision of infrastructure and later formalization of housing difficult.

This problem is exacerbated by the very slow conversion to designated new land use. Underuse of urban and rural land allocated through lease or rent, in particular, land allocated for investment purposes, is reportedly very common. For instance, according to recent media reports, the Addis Ababa city administration had to repossess land from investors who failed to begin construction projects, even though land had been allocated more than four years ago. Backing this observation, experts estimate that, countrywide, of the land use assignments that were changed during the past three years, only 30 percent actually occurred in practice. Mechanisms that would allow the public to capture a significant share of the gains from changing land use are also lacking. Although the level of infrastructure development is considered as a factor in determining land use or land rent payment rates to the government, failure to update valuation benchmarks that form the basis for rent determination has rendered this tool ineffective. Different areas or zones in Addis Ababa were last rated for calculating land rents in 1995, and the situation is not better in other towns or secondary towns.

With the exception of building permits, few of the restrictions regarding urban land use are regularly enforced. Building permits are a requirement for the allocation of cement for a building project. Such permits are affordable.[52] However, concerns have been raised about building permits being cheap compared to the cost of having public authorities process such permits. Although building permits are usually issued in a timely manner (less than three months), problems such as the failure to conduct exhaustive assessments on inspection visits, the inclusion of unknown directives and other guidelines in the permit notice (for example, maximum site coverage of residential buildings set at 75 percent through an interoffice memo), and weak monitoring once building permits have been issued may warrant attention.

The procedures between the acquisition of land and utility connection are bypassed because the necessary institutions anticipated by the substantive law are absent and because prevailing views on existing planning allow avoidance of such procedures. No standards are set for plot sizes, although the lease proclamation, in specifying that 73 square meters shall be granted for residential purposes, has set this as a benchmark. Transfer restrictions are also not followed, and widespread violations are reported to have occurred.

Land Taxation

In urban areas, there are two taxes on land: an annual land rent and an annual building tax. Land rent is paid by both permit holders and leaseholders and is in addition to the payments due under the lease agreements. Land rents paid to the government for land held under leases reflect a house valuation based on location and accessibility.[53] However, the factors used are often outdated (over 15 years old in Addis Ababa) and do not consider improvements. Land rents paid to the government for land held under the permit system are typically based on historical values and are well below market prices. This basis results in very low rents that do not reflect the economic values of properties and that suggest high public subsidies through allocation of land. The lease system does not solve the problem either: most leaseholders make only the minimum advance payment of 5 percent of the total lease value, and the systems to record leases and ensure that payments are correctly assessed and collected often do not function properly, leading to high levels of evasion. The valuation of property for the purpose of establishing tax rates is based on taxpayers' self-declared annual rentals, resulting in significant underdeclaration and underpayment.

At the same time, tax collection is efficient. In urban areas, the process of listing property for taxation purposes is integrated into the land allocation system, resulting in a low cost of collection. This observation suggests that tax rolls are normally complete. A widespread public perception that tax receipts provide evidence of rights suggests that even informal landholders who are not legally liable to pay taxes are eager to make tax payments. The result is high levels of collection that are estimated to range between 70 percent and 80 percent of assessed property taxes, especially in urban areas. In rural areas, land use taxes are collected together with the agricultural income tax, also resulting in low cost of collection. The main reason for noncollection is that the criteria used in a large number of exemptions are not always clearly based on equity or efficiency and are not always applied in a transparent and consistent manner.

With the exception of rental or lease agreements between private parties and concessions granted to investors on public land through auctions, rents that are paid by permit holders and lease payments by leaseholders are not determined in a free market. This situation, together with poor valuation methods, results in local governments forgoing large amounts of potential revenue from taxes (land rent and building tax) or leases.[54] This loss of revenue in turn curtails governments' ability to provide services and infrastructure. Because between 40 percent and 60 percent of municipal revenue is land related, the potential implications are far-reaching.

Land is granted to peasants and pastoralists without charge, other than a nominal annual land tax that depends on area only and is independent of location or land quality. With increased demand for agricultural land, lease payments by outside investors could potentially make a significant contribution to revenue. However, allocation of rural land to investors is typically based on a negotiated payment schedule with little reference to the proposed use or size of the investment, and lease payments bear little relationship to market values and are rarely determined by auction.[55] Regional governments' collection of revenues from investors is thus very low.[56]

Public Land Management

In Ethiopia, all land is public. In addition, a particular category of "state holding" is defined in the rural land law, and municipalities administer and manage lands used in their own context. With most land being managed by the state, the land administration system is critical to the government's ability to manage this asset both in an effective manner and in a way that represents all citizens' interests. Gaps can lead to loss of revenue and undermine transparency on a large scale, especially in areas subject to rapid urban expansion.

The Ethiopian constitution gives the federal government an overall mandate to manage public land and gives regional states a mandate to administer the same resources as under the federal laws. There are therefore laws concerning public land at both federal and regional levels. This overlap results in ambiguity in the assignment of responsibility for the management of public land, both among central agencies and between the different levels of government. However, because all land is owned by the state, the state has little incentive to manage its holdings, which results in poor management. Most reports indicate that wildlife reserves and game parks exist on paper only. The Gambella National Park has virtually ceased to exist as a conservation area, Yabello Sanctuary has been taken over by a livestock project, and Bale Mountains National Park has suffered from uncoordinated development in and near its boundaries.

The problem is exacerbated by the fact that state holdings are generally not mapped or recorded. Recording and demarcation of publicly held land in Addis Ababa and some regional states occurred in some cases by the end of the 1990s: Awash and Simen Mountains national parks were legally mapped, presumably after demarcation, and demarcation of the Omo and Mago national parks was completed in 2005. Resources for management of public land are largely allocated at the regional and municipal levels, with the federal government taking a limited role in relation to land it has designated for state holding. However, the financial and human resource capacities of regional states and municipalities appear to be far short of what is required to manage public land falling under their respective jurisdictions.

Regarding the disposal of land, land in rural areas is not auctioned; it is granted through negotiations upon request by an investor with a viable project proposal. In urban areas, under the leasehold system, land is generally auctioned for residential, manufacturing, commerce, and construction purposes. More than 97 percent of the land allocated under the leasehold system in Addis Ababa in the two years ending in May 2008 was allocated under a lottery or auction system. However, these auctions often involve a secretive, nontransparent bidding process, leading to wide variations in prices. In fact, nontransparent allocation of high-value land at the urban fringe through nonmarket mechanisms has also been identified as a major source of weak governance and conflict.

Expropriation mainly supports urban expansion and makes land available to private investors. A 2007 study covering selected rural sites revealed that more than one-third (almost 37 percent) of households compensated for expropriation lost their holdings for private investment or urban expansion. Though the total area of land expropriated within Addis Ababa is not available, about one-fourth (24 percent) of all allocations by the Addis Ababa city government in the two-year period ending May 2008 had been transferred for private purposes, among which was the large-scale conversion of agricultural land in expansion areas into housing cooperatives. Experts estimated that, countrywide, more than 50 percent of the land expropriated in the past three years is used for private purposes.

Adequate provisions in the expropriation procedure require, prior to clearance, the identification of the recipient as the party responsible for compensation. Because the recipient is presumably eager to begin the planned venture as soon as possible, transfer is actively sought and expedited as soon as compensation payments are handled. Moreover, current investment and land use laws require that land be used for its intended purpose within a set time limit, and they mandate that the state take back allocated land if it is not used for that purpose within the set period of time. Land is quickly expropriated, and most expropriated land is used for the intended purpose within three years.

In most rural and urban areas, compensation for expropriation involves land as well as monetary compensation and, except in medium-size towns, is timely. Land-to-land compensation is not available in cases in which investors who will gain access to the land are responsible for compensation. Thus, though this arrangement has reportedly facilitated timely payment of compensation, it has also created landlessness among peasant communities that have no possibility to use the money they received to purchase land elsewhere. However, although mechanisms exist to provide informal settlers with a minimum-size plot of land without the payment of any monetary compensation, the law requires compensation only for registered landholders. There is no legal right to compensation for loss of land rights as a result of the conversion of rural land into urban land or the transformation of land from communal use to protected areas.

Although federal laws mandate establishment of land clearance and appeal commissions, few commissions have been established outside of Addis Ababa. Even there, the land clearance appeal commission has only one office, making it inaccessible to most residents. Its effective operation is hampered by limited human resources as well as jurisdictional disputes with the municipality courts, which lead to lengthy delays before courts reach a decision. The situation is further complicated by attempts to resolve the backlog of cases through a standardized format that has favored the government party. Instead of resolving the problem, this initiative has led to the filing of appeals in almost every case.

Public Provision of Land Information

Rural land certification in Ethiopia's four main regions is one of the largest and most cost-effective land registration programs worldwide. Over a period of three to five years, the initiative has registered some 25 million parcels. It has been implemented effectively and in a participatory, pro-poor, and gender-sensitive manner. The program significantly departs from the approach of the traditional land titling interventions in a number of ways: (a) by issuing usufruct rights certificates rather than full titles; (b) by promoting gender equity with joint land ownership; (c) by using a participatory, decentralized process of field adjudication; and (d) by using low-cost community identification of boundaries. All of this helped establish the basis for a low-cost land administration system in rural areas.

The cost of registering a property transfer is low, particularly in rural areas. The only fees collected on rural land registration relate to certificate costs, and even these are waived for first-time registration in Amhara. Rural landholding certificates are issued to landholders for free in Amhara, for ETB 5 (US$0.60) in Oromia, and for ETB 2 (US$0.25) in SNNP. The direct costs of land registration have been calculated at about ETB 29.5 (US$3.50) per household, or ETB 8.3 (less than US$1.00) per plot, excluding the cost of the certificate and the annual maintenance cost once the cadastre is established. Registries operate as part of the general administration rather than on a self-sustaining basis. There is practically no capital investment in the rural land registration system, something that jeopardizes the financial sustainability of the registry.

For sustainability of the gains from first-stage certification in rural areas,[57] land records need to be properly maintained, in particular, those involving the registration of changes. Procedures specify that duplicate registry books be maintained at village (*kebele*) and district (*woreda*) levels, but lack of registry books by many *kebeles* requires travel to the *woreda* to make changes. The type of books of possession issued to landholders varies widely across regions, with some being parcel based and some being holding based. Agreement on a common computerized system is lacking, and fundamental questions remain unresolved. No clear procedures exist for updating records, and neither registry books nor landholding certificates are structured in a way that would facilitate recording of changes in rights over time.[58] There are no clear rules on when and how registers must be updated (for example, inheritance or short-term transfer) or what sanctions may be incurred if that is not done. This lack of requirements suggests that no information is available on recorded (or actual) transactions.

Because none of the regions have developed ways to prepare cadastral maps on a large scale, rural land records lack a spatial reference. Neither private encumbrances nor public restrictions are recorded, and the records in the registry can be searched only by holder name. Although some rural areas have ad hoc standards relating to requirements for services and a time frame for service provision, there is no evidence of their publication. Instead, customers are normally informed of applicable standards at the time of their request. Even where individual rights have been registered, little, if any, of the land held under communal tenure has been mapped and recorded, which reportedly gives rise to significant encroachment.

Given the lack of a formal urban registration system, registration in urban centers is normally linked to the provision of land for new holdings or transfer of ownership for existing holdings. Cadastral plans often identify parcels on A4-size plans prepared in AutoCAD that are printed and appended to the file or, in the case of Addis Ababa, are printed directly on the title certificate. Though the practice is not consistent, municipalities in major towns mainly keep ledger books (registers) for transfers, mortgages, and title deeds separately. Urban ledger books for title deeds, the nearest thing to a register in some of the urban centers, are stored as files for each property identified by a physical address. Private encumbrances, if registered at all, are thus listed in separate documents, and the fact that registers are held separately from each other without clear cross-referencing makes it difficult for third parties to access them.

The extent of timely access to relevant urban property records varies across urban areas as well as institutions within the same municipality. Although authenticated copies of title deeds and transfer contracts are swiftly provided upon request in Addis Ababa, other municipalities without computerized systems have cumbersome procedures that take significantly more time. Misplacement or even loss of files is also a serious problem in municipalities and semiurban areas. Available information indicates that service standards exist only for a few aspects related to property registration in urban areas. Even these incomplete standards are rarely published and may change at any time without notice.

In urban areas, information on land rights is available to interested institutions upon written request at no cost. But the absence of relevant information, such as encumbrances over property, makes it very difficult to access land information in practice. Registration fees can be obtained by asking, although they depend on property values. Only intermediaries can obtain copies or extracts of documents, which usually takes more than a month. Mechanisms to handle complaints on land registration include the Office of the Ombudsman at federal and regional levels, as well as complaint committees in most major towns and in rural areas. Because these operate outside the registry system, there is little monitoring of staff in the registry or proactive systems to discourage illegal activity by registry staff.

The costs of adding a title plan to a certificate is about ETB 250 (US$30). Similarly, the only fees directly related to registration are rather low, at ETB 45 (US$4) per registered property. In urban areas, an additional stamp duty of 2 percent of property value must be paid. Given widespread underdeclaration of property values, actual amounts paid are low, contributing to insufficient capital investment in the system.

Dispute Resolution

Despite a system of village-level courts to complement first-instance courts at the *woreda*, access to justice is difficult. Judges are often ill-informed, because it is difficult to obtain copies of regional legislation for purchase. Courts can be physically distant, especially from pastoral communities and peripheral areas; are often not functional; and may refuse to hear arguments in nonofficial regional languages. Where formal conflict resolution institutions are not functional, as well as in the lowlands, traditional and religious dispute resolution mechanisms have become the most important dispute mechanisms to replace the formal justice system. Decisions of these entities are recognized by the formal system. However, decisions by the traditional elders at the local level may not always be equitable or gender sensitive.

Parallel avenues for conflict resolution also exist, with a number of alternative forums available, including land administration boards, land clearance appeals commissions, municipal courts, regional courts, federal courts, and other institutions with adjudication mandates. There is no mechanism to share information, so collaboration between these institutions is very limited and often informal. As a result, three or four venues may entertain the same case at the same time, especially when one of the parties has the resources. In litigation on land issues, decisions at the first-instance court normally tend to favor the government. Courts are clogged with long-standing land disputes. This backlog is exacerbated by parties lodging parallel actions. It is estimated that land disputes in Ethiopia constitute between one-third and one-half of all cases within the formal justice system. Overlap also occurs between different conflict resolution institutions at different administrative levels and in cases of outside investment.

Policy Recommendations

Policy recommendations for Ethiopia have identified the necessity to provide guidelines for the implementation of federal laws, to have harmonized and realistic restrictions on land rights, to strengthen the legal recognition of women's rights to rural land, to review participatory process in land policy and legislation, to design federal policies of formalization, to create a federal institution for land valuation, to consistently consider land values when land is transferred, to establish a complete mapping of land types, to ensure sustainability of the land registration system, and to improve local capacity.

Guidelines for Implementation of Federal Laws

Although land legislation is the mandate of the federal government, key policy choices have been delegated to regional states. However, detailed guidelines on how federal laws, proclamations, regulations, or directives are to be implemented, and the hierarchy of legislation, are missing. There is no monitoring of implementation, precluding an assessment of the degree of adherence to policies and the reasons for this adherence. An institution to monitor implementation of key laws and regulations in a uniform and consistent manner would be desirable.

Nature of and Restrictions on Land Rights

In rural areas, some of the restrictions on land use by peasants may be difficult to justify or implement consistently. For example, limiting inheritance to family members actually living on the land may run counter to the land policy's equity and nondiscrimination objectives and may stymie development of the nonagricultural economy. Constraints on the share of land that can be leased out may similarly limit incentives for investment and nonfarm employment. In fact, despite the existence of land registration, urban residents have, in practice, rights that are more robust than those of their rural counterparts. A review of land transfer restrictions is warranted, with a view to ensuring rural-urban equity in landholding rights, and in light of experience thus far. In urban areas, land use restrictions often are not enforced because laws may be conflicting. Injunctions to protect the possessory rights of persons found in violation of land use legislation are also a serious issue. Though this issue can be sustainably resolved only through a review of the 1960 civil code, its potentially irreversible impact calls for immediate resolution through specific legislation. Such legislation may also consider harmonizing adjudicatory mandates among judicial bodies at the federal, regional, and municipal levels.

Recognition of Women's Rights to Rural Land

Though the rights of women to have access to land on equal footing with men have been explicitly stated in the relevant federal and regional laws, and major strides to secure these rights have been made through rural land certification, two gaps remain. One is that laws in Oromia and SNNP do not clearly address the rights of women in polygamous unions. A second gap is that laws promoting female equality are limited to agrarian contexts, and guidelines are lacking for women's rights in the context of communal landholdings in pastoral areas. A review of rural land use legislation at all levels is recommended to clarify the status of the women's land use rights, together with follow-up actions to encourage effective exercise of these rights (for example, through female participation on land certification committees).

Participatory Decision Making on Land Issues

Though highly desirable, decentralization in the design and implementation of land policy, legislation, and land use planning has not led to the expected levels of public participation. Thus, a review of the decision-making processes relating to land issues in light of federal policy on local government and decentralization will be useful. This effort should include a review of the extent to which equity and nondiscrimination in land policy and legislation can be mainstreamed and integrated into existing policy frameworks. It can be combined with an assessment of the results of the implementation of rural land policy thus far and the suggestion of monitoring indicators for the future.

Formalization in Urban Areas and Prevention of Informality in Rural Areas

Informality, through squatting and nonformalized holding rights, is a problem of increasing importance for land use and policy in Addis Ababa and other towns. Yet, efforts to address the problem have been limited and piecemeal, often in the context of ad hoc measures that lacked clarity and uniformity. Given the size of the problem, it would be more appropriate to address the issue through policy decisions at the federal level. Informal settlement by peasants in forestland or other public land is also likely to become a serious challenge to rural land use, and policy measures to address the problem at an early stage are needed, preferably at the federal level.

Property Valuation Institution

Gaps and problems in property valuation are widespread. A contributing factor is the absence of a uniform system of land valuation in line with Ethiopia's land tenure system. This uniformity can best be achieved by creating a specialized institution to set guidelines for land and property valuation in urban and rural areas. Such an institution would be most effective if supported by legislative provisions at the federal level. Moreover, to the extent that the current infrastructure-based valuation system is to be maintained in urban areas, the outdated studies used as the basis for valuation need to be updated.

Transfers to Take Into Account Land Value Consistently

A key factor underlying the discrepancies between the land rent and taxation systems and the market is the fact that land value is not taken into account in assessing the value of properties. Though apparently consistent with public policy considerations, the current system is unrealistic. Such deficiencies are particularly serious for compensation and relocation assistance in cases of clearance and expropriation. Mechanisms to base these cases on market values are a priority. Also, although laws provide for compensation for clearance of land in rural areas, current practice has led to uncompensated clearance of peasants in some areas because of a failure to clearly identify the party responsible for payment of compensation. Analysis of the gaps is recommended, with identification of immediate measures to protect peasants having to clear their landholdings for urban expansion.

Complete Mapping of Publicly, Privately, and Communally Held Land

Although land certification had very positive effects in terms of perceived tenure security and female empowerment, incomplete registers and maps reduce its effectiveness. Efforts to put in place cadastres in urban areas are encouraging, but they should be comprehensive (covering state, private, and communal land) and clearly linked to land rights. Also, because many problems with the current land use planning and policy framework can be traced in part to absence of comprehensive and up-to-date land use information, prompt compilation of such information (including up-to-date benchmarks for valuation) is needed. Finally, there is need to ensure that institutions using land-related information share databases to avoid duplication of effort and confusion. In land dispute adjudication, absence of a mechanism to share information led to extensive forum shopping and parallel processes. Establishment of a networking system such as the one between police, prosecution, and courts in criminal cases is recommended.

Sustainability of the Rural Land Registration System

Ensuring the sustainability of rural land registration requires at least a minimum level of investment in equipment and human resources for maintenance. Such investment will need to be linked to monitoring of registry performance and establishment of financing arrangements (for example, clear user fees and possibly some cross-subsidies from urban areas) to ensure sustainability of the registration system at federal, regional, and local levels. Federal standards can greatly reduce the cost of such maintenance.

Strengthening of Local Governance

A very positive aspect of the current land administration system is its high level of decentralization. However, though authority for most decisions rests at the local level, guidance to inform officials at *woreda* and village levels is lacking. Defining local governance structures, roles, and mandates in land governance should be considered. Because limited capacity of local implementing structures at the local level is a pervasive problem, building the capacities of these structures should continue to be a policy priority. Capacity-building efforts should also be considered by putting in place the necessary federal and regional laws, regulations, and guidelines as well as making technical support available.

INDONESIA

Indonesia, with a population of 230 million, had a formerly highly centralized system that has been reformed over the past decade to become highly decentralized, while land functions remain highly centralized. With 33 provinces, significant power devolved to districts and municipalities. Indonesia also illustrates the challenges of a country faced with management issues regarding its significant forest and natural resources and the problems that may be associated with legal pluralism, that is, the coexistence of the national state law with customary laws (*adat*) that govern Indonesia's traditional communal land tenure system. In this context, many opportunities exist for Indonesia to overcome obstacles that prevent economic actors from gaining more secure rights to land and, thus, for society to fully benefit from the advantages of land as a safety net and to respond to incentives for sustainable management and investment.

Recognition and Enforcement of Rights

Land tenure (see tables 4.6 and 4.7) is regulated by the 1960 Basic Agrarian Law (BAL) that provides legal recognition of many different tenure types, including individual registrable rights of ownership (*Hak Milik*), plantation (*Hak Guna Usaha*), building (*Hak Guna Bangunan*), or use (*Hak Pakai*). The BAL also recognizes nonregisterable rights, including communal ones (*Hak Ulayat*), under customary law.

Despite the recognition of a broad range of rights, three factors lead to considerable uncertainty of rights. First, and most important, the scope of the BAL is extremely limited in practice because it applies to only approximately 30 percent of the country's land area that is not classified as forestland.[59] Formally designated forestland, which represents almost 70 percent of the total land in Indonesia, is managed by the Ministry of Forestry, although large parts of the forestland are degraded and no longer carry trees. Because only temporal concessions and no tenure rights can be obtained on forestland, communities that may have been living on the land for a long time often find themselves with no legally recognized rights to such land. The difficulty of achieving formal recognition of communal property rights on forestland perpetuates tenure insecurity.

Second, even though the BAL dates from the 1960s, while many regulations to enforce certainty of land rights have been promulgated, there have been little efforts to enforce them at the grassroot levels (for example, lack of training or absence of a reliable mechanism to disseminate new regulations and monitor their enforcement). For example, because the BAL does not contain regulations for the recognition of group rights, and in spite of attempts to pass regulations confering rights to groups, groups that want to have their rights legally recognized are de facto required to individualize them. Doing so will significantly increase the cost of demarcation and may be in line with neither local visions and aspirations nor actual land use patterns. More important, although in practice individualization is required, the process to actually formalize individual land tenure is lengthy and can be expensive. Furthermore, communal tenure exists on land administered by the National Land Agency (*Badan Pertanahan Nasional* [BPN]) and on forestland administered by the Ministry of Forestry, and other sectoral agencies (including mines and energy) issue concessions or permits over such land. Taken together, the multiplicity of ill-defined rights and institutional responsibilities means that different types of rights are frequently superimposed, which presents challenges for their enforcement and provides an environment that is conducive to the emergence of conflicts.

Table 4.6 Tenure Typology for Indonesia, Urban Sector

Tenure type	Legal recognition and characteristics	Issues and potential overlaps
Land under the control of the National Land Office		
State land	Legal recognition: By constitution Registration/recording: Possible Transferability: Application by eligible parties to the state through the relevant land office	In principle, all land is controlled by the state. In practice, land that is not zoned as forest and that has no existing title (other than for the state) is state land. *Control* includes the authority to regulate land use and make it available to private parties. Once a plot of land is state land, it should be possible for the person who has possession over it or who can prove possession or chain of possession over it, to apply for registered titles (*Hak Milik, Hak Guna Bangunan, Hak Guna Usaha*, or *Hak Pakai*, as discussed below). To be converted to certificated (registered) title, land with noncertificated (nonregistered) title (for example, *adat* land held individually) must have its title relinquished, must revert to the state (technically becoming state land), and must have a new application made for land rights to be issued with certificated title.
Registered and certificated private ownership	Legal recognition: Basic Agrarian Law (BAL) 1960 Registration/recording: Possible Transfer: To eligible parties	*Hak Milik*, a right of ownership, provides the most comprehensive land right in Indonesia. *Hak Milik* is transferable and inheritable and can be the subject of security. It can be held only by Indonesian citizens and, under very limited circumstances, certain Indonesian bodies (for example, banks). A *Hak Milik* is a primary title and can be encumbered by the grant of secondary land rights (see below).

(continued next page)

Table 4.6 (Continued)

Tenure type	Legal recognition and characteristics	Issues and potential overlaps
Registered and certificated private possession and use	Legal recognition: BAL Registration/recording: Possible Transfer: To eligible parties for specified use only	The most common use right is *Hak Guna Bangunan* (HGB; the right to construct and use buildings on nonowned land), a renewable 30-year right for citizens and legal entities incorporated and domiciled in Indonesia. *Hak Pakai* is a right of use on state land that is not owned. HGB can be held by Indonesian companies and foreign individuals and companies. *Hak Pakai* can be held by foreign citizens domiciled in Indonesia and foreign corporate bodies having representation in Indonesia. Each title is granted for different time periods. HGB can be extended. A *Hak Pakai* can be granted indefinitely for a specific use and will lapse once that use comes to an end. It can also be granted for a limited period of years for unspecified use. HGB and *Hak Pakai* can be granted as primary titles on state land or as secondary titles on *Hak Milik*. Where such titles have been created as a secondary title, their continued existence will depend on continuation of the primary title and the relevant terms of the agreement under which the secondary title was created. Transferability of each title depends on its characteristics, use, and the identity of the transferee.
Unregistered private ownership (possession and control)	Legal recognition: Regulation No. 24 of 1997 on Land Registration Registration/recording: Possible Transferability: Possible	Documentary nonregistered evidence of possession such as agreements to transfer or relinquish title or a power of attorney is recognized and can be registered with suitable documentary evidence. Without such evidence, and under specific conditions, ownership can be registered following physical possession for more than 20 years.

Unregistered ownership by government agencies	Legal recognition: BAL; Reg. No. 24/1997; Reg. No. 11/2010 (National Land Agency) Registration/recording: Possible Transferability: s.t. criteria	State companies or regional governments often claim ownership and control of land without documentary evidence of title. The entity that has ownership or control of the land is frequently unclear. A 2004 law requires that land controlled by the central or regional government must be registered. Transfer of such land must then be carried out with approval of the minister of finance and the relevant ministry.
Unregistered occupation and use of land	Legal recognition: BAL; Reg. No. 24/1997; Reg. No. 11/2010 Registration/recording: No Transferability: No	People frequently occupy land, most commonly state land, but also privately owned land (for example, on the boundary of a factory or power station). Under specific conditions, ownership can be registered following physical possession of the land for more than 20 consecutive years.
Abandoned land	Legal recognition: BAL; Reg. No. 24/1997; Reg. No. 11/2010 Registration/recording: Possible Transferability: No	Abandonment of a plot of land for a certain period of time may lead to the termination of the title vested upon the land. The head of the National Land Office has the authority to determine whether a plot is abandoned. This will include cancellation of the relevant title and categorization of the land as state land. The public use of the land will be determined by the head of the National Land Office.
Land under the control of the Ministry of Forestry		
Unpermitted use of forestry-zoned land	Legal recognition: No Registration/recording: No Transferability: No	In some urban and peri-urban areas, houses and commercial buildings have encroached on land zoned as forestland. Where land is zoned as forest, it is not legally possible for a land title to be granted, regardless of the fact that no trees exist on the land and that buildings have been constructed.

Source: Various sources; compiled by U. Meades.

Note: BAL = Basic Agrarian Law 1960; HGB = *Hak Guna Bangunan*; s.t. = strata title (condominium).

Table 4.7 Tenure Typology for Indonesia, Rural Sector

Tenure type	Legal recognition and characteristics	Issues and potential overlaps
Land under the control of the National Land Agency		
State land	Legal recognition: By constitution Registration/recording: Possible Transferability: Application by eligible parties to the state through the relevant land office	In principle, all land is controlled by the state. This is very common in rural areas with land often overlapping areas claimed by *adat* communities as ancestral land. The difficulties of recognizing *adat* land rights suggest that, in the past, registered title was often on *adat* lands and land claimed by *adat* communities may be treated as available for grant of title by the land office. In certain circumstances, *Hak Pengelolaan* (right to manage), derived from the state's authority to control land, can be granted as a primary title to government or agencies. It is not generally transferable, but secondary rights can be issued on its basis.
Registered and certificated private ownership	Legal recognition: Basic Agrarian Law (BAL) 1960 Registration/recording: Possible Transfer: To eligible parties	*Hak Milik*, a right of ownership, provides the most comprehensive land right in Indonesia. *Hak Milik* is transferable and inheritable and can be the subject of security. It can be held only by Indonesian citizens and, under very limited circumstances, certain Indonesian bodies (such as banks). A *Hak Milik* is a primary title and can be encumbered by the grant of secondary land rights.

Registered and certificated private possession and use	Legal recognition: BAL Registration/recording: Possible Transfer: To eligible parties for specified use only	The most common use right is *Hak Guna Bangunan* (HGB; the right to construct and use buildings on nonowned land), a renewable 30-year right for citizens and legal entities incorporated and domiciled in Indonesia. *Hak Pakai* is a right of use on state land that is not owned. HGB can be held by Indonesian companies and foreign individuals and companies. *Hak Pakai* can be hold by foreign citizens domiciled in Indonesia and foreign corporate bodies having representation in Indonesia. Each title is granted for different time periods. An HGB can be extended. A *Hak Pakai* can be granted indefinitely for a specific use and will lapse once that use come to an end. It can also be granted for a limited period of years for unspecified use. HGB and *Hak Pakai* can be granted as primary titles on state land or as secondary titles on *Hak Milik*. Where such titles have been created as a secondary title, their continued existence will depend on continuation of the primary title and the relevant terms of the agreement under which the secondary title was created. Transferability of each title depends on its characteristics, use, and the identity of the transferee.
Unregistered private ownership (possession and control)	Legal recognition: Regulation No. 24 of 1997 on Land Registration Registration/recording: Possible Transferability: Possible	Documentary nonregistered evidence of possession, such as agreements to transfer or relinquish title or a power of attorney, is recognized and can be registered with suitable documentary evidence. Without such evidence, and under specific conditions, ownership can be registered following physical possession for more than 20 years. In rural areas, significant uncertainty relating to evidence of title and land boundaries exists.

(continued next page)

Table 4.7 (Continued)

Tenure type	Legal recognition and characteristics	Issues and potential overlaps
Adat community on lands under Badan Pertanahan Nasional (BPN; Indonesian National Land Agency jurisdiction)	Legal recognition: BAL; Reg. No. 24/1997; Reg. No. 11/2010 (National Land Office) Registration/recording: Possible Transferability: s.t. criteria.	Many adat communities live and use land under the jurisdiction of the BPN. Provision exists for formal recognition and registration of adat land rights, but the procedure is complicated, and such rights are subject to statutory ownership (see below). For establishment of such rights, regulations require determination whether adat rights still exist. The existence of adat land belonging to a specific adat community must be recorded on a land registration map showing the boundaries of the land and must be registered. The exercise of adat rights by communities excludes plots possessed by individuals or statutory bodies by virtue of a certified land title under BAL or plots acquired or appropriated by government institutions.
Individual adat rights	Legal recognition: BAL; Reg. No. 24/1997; Reg. No. 11/2010 Registration/recording: No Transferability: No	Individual adat rights are legally recognized but have limited relevance in practice.
Land under the control of the Ministry of Forestry		
Land zoned as forest	Legal recognition: Law 41/99 (Forestry Law) Registration/recording: No Transferability: No	In forest-zoned areas, three types of overlaps are common. First, many oil, gas, and mining concessions are granted over land that is zoned as forest. Though concessions do not convey land rights (which, as those for use and access, must be negotiated separately with the Ministry of Forestry), a lack of coordination among the relevant ministries (Energy and Mineral Resources vs. Forestry) often causes issuance of overlapping permits or granting of mining concessions in forest where mining is prohibited. Second, forestry and mineral permits and concessions are often issued with limited regard for existing land occupation and use. This has caused significant problems,

		because many communities, including *adat* ones, live and earn their livelihoods on forest-zoned land. Third, land title can be obtained legally only once land is released from forest zoning in a complicated and long process. But, in certain areas, titles have been issued over forest-zoned land.
Adat communities using land zoned as forest	Legal recognition: Law 41/99 Registration/recording: No Transferability: No	*Adat* communities frequently occupy and use forest-zoned land. The Forestry Law states that the use of *adat* forests by an *adat* law community may be carried out under certain conditions. However, the procedure can be cumbersome: the law requires verification of the existence of the *adat* community and the issue of a local government regulation confirming its existence.
Non-*adat* communities using forest-zoned land	Legal recognition: Minister of forestry Regulation No. P.37/Menhut-II/2007 on Community Forest (as amended)	Many non-*adat* communities occupy forest-zoned land and can obtain certain rights. A request for a permit to use an area as a community forest working area enables the governor or regent to propose that a specific forest area be designated as community forest working area. If approved, the minister of forestry issues a decree designating the area as community forest belonging to the specific community. Communities can then apply for a permit to the regent to carry out activities in the community forest. The procedure is cumbersome, however, and overlaps exist. A community forest can be designated in an area that is zoned as protected forest or production forest but only if no other right or permit, including a concession, has been granted.
Individuals using forest-zoned land	Legal recognition: Law 41/99 (Forestry Law) Registration/recording: No Transferability: No	It is not technically possible to obtain registered land title on forest-zoned land, although in certain areas of Indonesia this has occurred. From a legal perspective, land title can be obtained only after the land has been released from the forest zoning, in most cases a lengthy and complicated process.

Source: Various sources; compiled by U. Meades.

Note: BAL = Basic Agrarian Law 1960; BPN = Badan Pertanahan Nasional.

Third, though the BAL is neutral regarding gender, and in spite of past efforts to promote joint titling, the amount of land registered in women's names remains limited.[60] Improving the share of land held by women and gender awareness are not yet a key part of contemporary discussions on land administration and policies.

In urban areas, the legal framework recognizes titled individual properties as well as condominiums, for which appropriate arrangements to manage common property exist. Both can be registered, either individually or through strata title registration. Nevertheless, there are high levels of informality, with some informal settlements having existed for several generations with no formal status. Individual informal property recognized under traditional or customary rules may also be formalized and subsequently registered but the process does not involve recognition of group rights. Squatters seldom benefit from adverse possession. Although the BAL intended to act on statutory limitation on the size of land ownership, enforcement is weak. It is difficult for creditors to repossess land and other guarantees for loans in default (that is, foreclosure) without court intervention. This action is costly in the best of circumstances and is even more difficult in an environment in which courts are seen as favoring debtors and often not being impartial. It is thus not surprising that the cost of credit in Indonesia is very high by regional standards.

Regarding the enforcement of rights, nondocumentary forms of evidence are accepted as proof of rights where documentary evidence is not available and where long-term peaceful occupation can be used to claim rights. However, because processes for recognizing long-term occupation are highly discretionary, few such claims are recognized in practice. For registration and formalization, an efficient, community-supported systematic registration process was developed under the Land Administration Project. In 2008, the project had registered a cumulative total of approximately 2.2 million parcels (or 4.6 million parcels, including cases in which users paid their own processing fees). However, BPN has been unable to scale up the systematic registration program as planned, and it is estimated that, at most, 38 million of the 80–100 million land parcels in Indonesia are registered. The cost of formalizing title to existing buildings is high and unaffordable by the majority of the population. As regards sporadic registration, formal fees charged by BPN (that is, excluding notary fees) are less than 5 percent of the property value, but informal fees exist and are significantly higher than formal ones. Finally, it is worth noting that land registration in Indonesia may still be subject to some level of tenure insecurity, given that a registered record can be challenged by a third party without time limit. Anecdotal evidence suggests that even people in possession of a land title for more than 10 years could still lose their land because a third party successfully proved before a court its claim based on an informal transaction. Many land titles are considered to be defective in one way or another. Although minor defects may not undermine ownership security, they can create the basis for future conflict.

Policy and Institutional Framework

Since 1999, when the regional government law established a more decentralized government structure, provincial and district governments have held more powerful legal positions and have begun to demand more authority in determining land policy within their respective jurisdictions (except for forestland, which, at least in principle, remains centrally managed). A highly complex mix of a hierarchal and top-down system of development and spatial planning exists, with the central government retaining the authority to override locally made spatial plans for special areas that have been deemed strategic and nationally important. Although the BAL describes norms for spatial planning with regard to land, the complex nature of functions and mandates allocated among governmental agencies has created an impasse. Land administration agencies, which include BPN, the National Coordinating Agency for Surveying and Mapping, the Ministry of Agriculture, and the Ministry of Forestry, are fragmented, with large overlaps and a tendency to perform land registrations and mapping largely for their own interests. With branches of each agency at national and provincial levels, overlaps are common, and activities often are assigned to individuals lacking skills. Lack of clear assignment of judicial authority and sectoral approaches to land management and administration result in inconsistent and discretional application of policy, especially regarding the administration of rights to forestland, and coordination between sector agencies remains limited.

Indonesian land policy is derived from existing legislation as well as from memos providing technical guidance for policy implementation. A highly sectoral and compartmentalized approach that differentiates between land administration, land use management, and state forestland management (the latter not covered under the previous categories) results in inconsistencies in policy. No effort is made to reconcile these inconsistencies. Under this sectoral approach, *adat*, or customary laws and interests, are largely ignored in practice. Though BPN reports on implementation of its responsibilities under the BAL, the extent of such reporting is limited and often inconsistent. Public participation, particularly on land acquisition and spatial management, is guaranteed by law, but it often is unclear how this input will be incorporated into actual decisions, especially as regards forestry.

Land Use Planning and Taxation

Relevant legislation establishes a hierarchal system of land use planning, and detailed city plans exist to guide urban development in major metropolises such as Jakarta. However, implementation is expensive and difficult to enforce. Quite a number of regions (districts), including the new ones that resulted from administrative fragmentation, have yet to formulate and promulgate their own spatial planning documents. Different sectors (forestry, public works, trade and industry, and tourism) may also devise their own development and land use planning. These may differ from the spatial planning documents made by the regional development planning boards at the provincial and district levels. It is also unclear how the BPN mandate to formulate land use policies connects to regional spatial planning documents. Changes in land use plans, many of them initiated by private commercial interests, are made frequently and without proper public notice. In some cases, such changes are made ex post to bring plans into accordance with actual land use on the ground rather than the opposite.

Restrictions on land use (zoning in urban and rural areas, protected areas, protection of archeological sites or historic buildings, and so forth) are largely based on public interest but are poorly enforced. Changes in land use are made difficult by a permit process whereby land use must conform to what is specified in the title, and any change of land use requires de facto a reversion to the state and a new grant of land rights. This process introduces an enormous element of bureaucratic discretion that can be perceived as an invitation to corruption and mismanagement. In general, building codes (including sanitary and safety regulations) are applied only to government buildings and constructions by commercial enterprises, which need permits from the local government. The forms to submit an application for land use change or to apply for building and construction permits are readily available in local government offices or on the Internet. However, the majority of the population living in urban areas or those living in the poorer quarters of the city tend to disregard any regulation that imposes limitations on land use (zoning regulations and building codes), resulting in widespread residential informality. Broad intervention and control over land by the state has given rise to considerable dissatisfaction among local populations.

Powers to tax property are clearly defined and distributed between central, provincial, and local governments. The central government, represented by provinces, administers the tax in return for 10 percent of the revenue. The remaining 90 percent is returned to districts (64.8 percent), provinces (16.2 percent), and the central government (10.0 percent). As a result of the districts' share, coverage[61] and property tax collection rates are high, and the tax is buoyant, because actual collection always exceeds targets based on previous years' collection. Exemptions are in line with policy considerations based on principles of equity and efficiency. However, the use of a very large set of variables to value properties results in a process that is often perceived as being complex and having little relationship to market prices. Under the prevailing tax law, the valuation rolls are not publicly available, and the information on a particular assessed property value can be obtained only by the concerned taxpayer. Sales prices are underdeclared, with most deeds stating a sale price a little above the "value of the tax object," which is not surprising because seller and purchaser must pay a 4 percent and 5 percent transfer tax, respectively, based on the declared price. Given the broad tax base (a total of about 75 million parcel holders), the potential of land taxes to support local government and to encourage efficient land use could be better met.

Management of Public Land

All land for which ownership or use cannot be proved is presumed to be state land. However, the way that the state currently plans land use or manages state land does not prevent either large-scale underuse of valuable land or speculative accumulation of nonproductive land holdings. BPN, as the national land agency, formulates, coordinates, and implements national land policies and programs; supervises land administration; controls and oversees land use restrictions; and is in charge of land demarcation and mapping. But its authority is limited by the dualism in administration of land (between state land and state forestland), suggesting that BPN presently may manage only approximately 30 percent of the whole land territory. BPN has no jurisdiction over the management and administration of land within the area assigned as state forestland by the Ministry of Forestry. Although BPN was created in 1988, mechanisms for its coordination with other agencies (for instance regarding land data sharing) remain to be rolled out on a broader scale.

Little information on state land is publicly available, and district and municipal governments and other government services lack data on the amount of state land placed under their control. In a number of prominent cases, use of state land differs from its intended use, and sometimes, such land has been converted to private use (such as public parks used as residential areas).

In general, the government does not lease out state land. However, it is possible for private individuals or corporations to hold a right to construct and possess buildings on state land (*Hak Guna Bangunan*), a right to cultivate on state land (*Hak Guna Usaha*) or a right to use state land (*Hak Pakai*). Holders of those land titles are taxed. However, as regards state forestland, the Ministry of Forestry possesses the authority to rent out forestland to plantations. Forestland is then converted to other uses. In addition, the Ministry of Forestry may also enter into public-private partnerships to manage national parks. However, the inability to award tenure or ownership rights in forest areas limits the amount of capital the forestry industry can raise, prompts concession holders to mine the land with little consideration for long-term sustainability, and leaves local communities with little opportunity to participate in revenue streams from resources.

The rule, although mostly disregarded in practice, is that land may only be expropriated if the intended use by the government for public interest accords with existing spatial (land use) plans. Spatial plans, based on local government deliberations, putatively provide the justification for public land transfer. Although owners of titled land may receive full compensation, less is offered to those holding land on the basis of tax receipts or under customary law. Squatters and illegal occupants, even if they occupy public land peacefully for a number of years and in some cases several generations, are not eligible to receive compensation. For those eligible, delays in making compensation payment are frequent, often because of disputes over the level of compensation. Lack of knowledge about appeals procedures and lack of independence in responding to complaints are responsible in part for delays. In addition, the fairness of compulsory acquisition has been contested.

Land Information and Land Administration

BPN is investing resources to develop the registration system and to roll out systematic registration. However, even for registered properties, the nature of recorded land information remains deficient. Less than half the registered properties are identifiable on maps, and links to the cadastre (land tax) maps are still at the level of pilots. The cost for registering property transfer is fixed (Property Tax Law No. 12/1994 and Government Regulation No. 46/2003) and below 1 percent of the property value, but there are additional charges. The parties to a transfer agreement must pay a fixed transfer charge of Rp 25,000 (about US$2.90) plus a 4 percent charge, and the buyer must pay a further charge of 5 percent (duty to be paid for title transfer and value added tax). The cost of transferring land in Indonesia is one of the highest in the region, suggesting that a large number of efficiency-enhancing land transactions will not take place or will be driven into informality, with all the negative consequences.

BPN has the sole authority to manage the land registry system through its land offices in the regions. Most of the records are paper based. The complexity of regulations governing first-time registration and land transactions results in cumbersome and poorly compiled property registration dockets. The completeness and reliability of BPN data vary widely. In Jakarta, 80 percent of land is titled and information digitized. In other major cities in Java, the records are less complete. In outer regions, the coverage is very low. In line with this pattern, for Jakarta and other big cities, BPN provides a search service by parcel and title holder. But nationwide, one can undertake only a manual search of the records by land certification registration number. Only owners of land or those with powers of attorney may obtain copies or extracts of documents. Only the tax office and the police are authorized by law to obtain detailed information on land holdings. The high level of informality affects reliability of BPN records negatively, especially through subsequent transactions.

BPN has an adequate practice of publicity in case of first-time registration (Regulation No. 24/1997) that gives other third parties time to submit an objection against the application for registration or to supply any other relevant information that may make registration impossible. There are meaningful published service standards, and the registry makes known the process and procedures for obtaining certain services, a price list, and an estimation of time required to complete the service. However, the registry does not actively monitor its performance against these standards, and it has not been fully effective in preventing illicit requests for additional money to speed up processes or to bypass certain formal requirements. Thus, in practice, many BPN officials do not follow standard procedures.

Dispute Resolution

Both formal and informal arrangements are in place in Indonesia to address land-related conflicts. Four different institutions possess parallel and overlapping competencies to handle land-related conflicts: the civil court, the criminal court, the administrative courts, and a dispute settlement forum established by BPN to handle disputes relating to land misadministration and errors in land registration or titling. BPN was also active in creating directives (Ministerial Regulation No. 5/1999) that provide guidance on how to settle conflicts regarding communal land. In some cases, BPN has been party to the dispute, impairing its ability to handle and settle disputes. Available tools to manage and resolve land conflicts appear to treat the symptoms rather than the causes, such as the lack of coordination among agencies and policies.

Because the formal dispute resolution system favors government agencies, dispute resolution mechanisms are even less effective in settling disputes with the state, particularly the Ministry of Forestry regarding forest planning and land use. Formal justice is available principally in district capital cities. However, access to justice is not equally distributed. Geographical conditions, costs, or lack of familiarity with procedures are a barrier. The long-standing perception that courts are not impartial has fueled society's distrust of the judiciary and police. Clear procedural regulations are in place and outline the right to appeal and bring a dispute to a higher court. However, making an appeal is costly and time consuming and is not readily affordable to the majority of people.

Policy Recommendations

Policy recommendations for Indonesia cover the necessity to strengthen land rights, to redefine institutional responsibilities, to better coordinate spatial planning, to reinforce the capacity for local land management, to improve land information quality, and to make service delivery more transparent.

Land Rights Recognition

A number of issues regarding land rights should be addressed. First, giving more explicit legal recognition to possession is desirable. Recognizing occupancy (possession) as evidence of land ownership and accepting informal evidence, such as tax receipts combined with testimony by neighbors, could greatly increase tenure security for poor people, help formalize millions of informal land transfers (and, thus, eliminate an enormous source of conflict), and improve incentives for investment in the large areas that formal land registration efforts will not be able to cover in the foreseeable future. Community land ownership is a second area for action. Allowing communities to own land, provided they conform to minimum levels of accountability, could help ward off intrusion by outsiders, increase investment incentives, and be compatible with a transition toward individual title in cases in which that is the most appropriate option. In this context, in addition to acceptance of traditional laws (*adat*) as a basis of evidence for land claims, recognition of a range of occupation and use patterns (for example, before and after a concession has been granted, once logging has been completed, and in conversion forest), including secondary uses, can significantly strengthen *adat* and provide a basis for land use regulations. Examples include requiring that certain land remains forest, linking property rights to responsibilities for sustainable management of land and forest, and defining landowners' entitlements to timber resources once concessions expire. Concession holders would have the opportunity to become landowners through purchase of land to which no prior entitlements exist, and agreements between the concession holder and local communities could allow the latter to negotiate terms of harvesting subject to the forest management law and, thus, more effectively share in resource benefits. This recommendation will require that the issue of forestland ownership be addressed. Giving secure tenure to such land can provide a key incentive for legitimate users to make long-term investments. Demarcation and registration of forestland is also critical to help protect public assets and to provide the basis for effective management and land use planning by the state.

Institutional Structure

Given the confusion from institutional overlaps, a single government agency (that is, BPN), should be responsible for administration, including registration, of public lands such as forest. The Ministry of Forestry's responsibility should be limited to managing public use of the land. Having only one agency responsible for the administration of all land would require a comprehensive inventory of all land, whether state or privately owned, that would have to be established and administered by a single agency. Management of land use could still be entrusted to expert line agencies. This assignment of responsibility would reduce duplication and make land administration more efficient, for example, by merging land and tax administration. It could also permit easier monitoring and enforcement of compliance. The responsibility for land management could remain with the ministries to separate land administration and management.

Spatial Planning

Similar to the recommendations for institutional structures, developing a national planning approach and coordinating existing spatial plans will ensure that land use planning is more transparent and public and that it is conducted at a local level. Focusing central efforts on defining clear performance criteria for land use while having detailed planning locally could lead to the establishment of coordinated and consolidated plans that would be more efficient and cost-effective. This approach also would allow zoning even in the many cases where cadastral maps are not currently available and are unlikely to become available in the foreseeable future. Redressing the lack of coordination and planning will require recognizing the ability of all owners to use land at their discretion subject to existing land use controls, ensuring community consultation, and making all plans publicly accessible at district (*kecamatan*) level. This approach will help to implement the autonomy law, to improve land allocation and accountability, and to establish comanagement approaches, with authority for decisions over land allocation resting at the local level, subject to consistency with this national approach to land use planning.

Local Land Management Capacity

Decentralization has greatly increased responsibilities of local governments. At the same time, resources (including facilities and staff) at their disposal to comply with obligations remain limited. One concern is that without extensive capacity-building programs for local governments, the local government simply will not be able to fulfill those responsibilities. To close the gap, the central government will need to support local governments in embarking on those functions and provide training and capacity building that will allow them to carry out those functions efficiently and transparently. Because the underfunding of land administration affects quality of service provision, an important aspect will be to use land taxation to pay for improved land delivery services. This expansion of services would require raising land taxes to realistic levels, based on the cost of providing land-related services and local tax needs, with the possibility of higher rates on unused land and exemptions for small and poor land owners. The national government could set maximum and minimum rates, eliminate tax breaks by local government, and manage horizontal redistribution. Land conversion tax and capital gains tax could be used in addition.

Quality of Land Information

At present, the value of land information is much reduced because such information is not complete and is often unreliable. A clear conveyancing law can help reduce the cost of transferring land and make registration a rule-based activity by setting standards and rules that transactions must follow, that control fraud and forgery, and that reduce opportunities for corruption. The law should allow for simplified, rapid processes for standard transfers (for example, inheritance and subdivision); establish publicity of records and transactions (such as by having witnesses certify transfers and requiring all surveys to become part of the public record); and clarify that forgery is void and that registration of forgery does not cure this defect. In this context, adoption of well-defined processes will allow registries to eliminate defective deeds over time and, thus, be a more viable option. Many other countries have put qualifications on titles that are legally uncertain or without survey and have established mechanisms that allow qualifications to be cured, either by passage of time or by production of a survey on demand, and with at least partial cost recovery. This option should be seriously explored. Combining supply-driven systematic registration with incentives for demand-driven, group-based registration could also help to empower the poor, to increase public confidence in registration, and to provide incentives to register.

Transparent Service Delivery

Establishing standards for land agencies, publicizing individual offices' success in meeting those standards, performing independent audits and complaint handling, and outsourcing where appropriate will all be key to improving provision of land information. In addition, the huge amount of alleged land-related improprieties makes it mandatory (a) to strictly enforce penalties for land-related frauds; (b) to honor the rights of victims to reclaim a loss from the offender or to be otherwise indemnified; (c) to declare invalid registrations that have been established fraudulently; and (d) to recognize liability, including the possibility of dismissal, by civil servants for errors and fraud committed under their watch. These standards can be widely publicized through dissemination campaigns to help reduce transaction costs, disputes, and tensions. Setting clear standards regarding service delivery fees charged (formal and informal) and appointing an independent agency to monitor handling of complaints will support this transparency. Finally, the current system for resolving land disputes is very slow and often offers no fair representation for the poor and disadvantaged groups. The government needs to establish a more efficient system of land dispute resolution, such as supporting a mediation mechanism at the local level and providing legal assistance to the poor and disadvantaged groups who are involved in land disputes with government agencies or commercial plantations. Resources should be identified, involving communities, technical staff at the subdistrict level, and local government. The information generated can be integrated with district-level spatial plans to identify areas of possible conflict that should receive priority attention.

NOTES

1. Peru has 28 regional governments, 194 provincial municipalities, and 1,834 district municipalities.
2. Through Law 24656, the General Law on Peasant Communities, the state recognizes the communities as fundamental democratic institutions, autonomous in their organization, communal activities, and land use, as well as regarding economic and administrative issues. The law (a) defines who may be community

members; (b) makes community lands inalienable; (c) establishes the minimum necessary quorums for decisions relevant to the community, such as selling the land; (d) establishes the land use and land tenure system within the community; (e) defines the functions and powers of the general assembly and the minimum quorums needed to make decisions; (f) describes the functions and roles of the communal directive and the minimum quorums for decision making; and (g) regulates the main features of the economic system and community enterprises.

3. Law 24657 details the procedures to establish the communal territory of communities whose borders are not identified unambiguously.

4. Law 26845 establishes the necessary procedures to enable villagers to personally acquire lands of the community.

5. Law 22175 deals with indigenous communities. It defines what constitutes a native community, including its membership and it regulates cadastral surveys and the entry of property titles in general. It also regulates the use of land in the forest and rainforest.

6. These figures are based on existing data complemented by approximations regarding percentages of formal properties and household structures. They do not exactly sum up to the total estimated Peruvian population.

7. Testimonies from neighbors are the typical example of nondocumentary forms of evidence in Peruvian legislation. In urban contexts, receipts of payment for public services or declarations of address to public authorities or private institutions can be used as forms of evidence (Article 38 of Supreme Decree 13-99-MTC on property formalization). In rural contexts, proofs of credit to finance investments in agriculture are also recognized (Article 41 of Supreme Decree 32-2008-VIVIENDA, Legislative Decree 1089, on proofs of possession).

8. For example, registrars must check civil status and require participation of both spouses in land transfers and mortgages. Acquisition of land rights by married individuals benefits the spouse even when she has not participated in the contract (Regulations for Inscription, Resolution No. 248-2008-SUNARP, Articles 14 and 15).

9. During the military junta administration led by Juan Velasco Alvarado (1968–75), a redistributive land reform ("land to the tiller") expropriated large tracts of land and handed them over to the peasant farmers (*campesinos*). The land reform's explicit objective was to end the rural socioeconomic structure by which the *campesino* class was exploited by the large landlords (*hacendados*). Therefore, the legal framework imposed maximum limits to land holdings, prevented corporate land ownership, and banned contracts that could be used to reproduce the exploitation scheme. Rather than subdividing the property, the reforms restructured many of the large estates as peasant farming cooperatives. Other large tracts of land were distributed among peasant farming communities (*comunidades campesinas*).

10. The titles lacking maps are deeds in which physical features of the local geography, along with directions and distances, are used to define and describe the boundaries of a parcel of land. Boundaries are described in prose, working around the parcel in sequence, from a point of beginning, and returning to the same point. It may include references to other adjoining parcels (and their owners). Typically, these descriptions lack standards, are very imprecise, and make reference to features of geography that—especially in rural areas—may change over time, like the course of a stream, the track of a road, a big tree, or a building. As a result, boundaries are imprecise, overlapping rights are very frequent, and the legal security that titles should offer is severely reduced. The situation is somewhat better for Andean

peasant farming communities, because only 1,959 of these (out of a total 6,082) still have such ill-defined boundaries.

11. For example, the Land Law (Law 26505), which liberalized the land market, and regulations on urban and rural property formalization (Legislative Decrees 667 and 803) explicitly set forth policy objectives to create the corresponding steward entities, to declare the reasons behind their decisions, and to set the expected outcomes.

12. For instance, the Ministry of Housing (National Housing Plan 2006-2015 "Housing for All") and the Ministry of Agriculture (Strategic Multi-annual Sector Plan of Agriculture 2007-2011) have published their multiyear plans, including an explicit diagnosis, expected outcomes, and the means to accomplish them. However, in neither case is it clear to what extent citizens were involved in preparing those policies or if indicators were monitored.

13. An example is the 2007 publication of a controversial article by the President, which noted that the country had too many resources "that cannot be transferred or receive investment, and do not generate jobs" (Garcia 2007). This statement led to a number of legislative decrees establishing mechanisms to promote better use of natural resources—forest, mining, and hydrocarbons—through private investment. The decrees in turn sparked a highly politicized national debate that led to massive demonstrations; violent conflict between indigenous communities and the police involving 39 deaths in June 2009; and, eventually, the abrogation of the decrees.

14. Housing policies concentrate on building of new homes mostly for the middle class, whereas formalization of settlements ends up being the housing policy for the poor. This system results in very inefficient uses of land. Many housing complexes promoted by the Ministry of Housing have been built without any coordination with local government authorities and sometimes disregard existing zoning plans.

15. These exemptions may be subjective (relating to the status of the property owners, such as pensioners and retirees, government agencies, universities and educational organizations, or political parties) or objective (relating to the status of the properties, such as part of a forest concession). Some experts consider that many exemptions introduce distortions. For example, exemptions for retirees are justified by the fact that retired pensions are very low; therefore, the inefficient administration of pension funds is charged to the local governments. The exemption of central government properties is justified in the lack of appropriate budgets of government agencies, which are subsidized by local governments, whereas the inefficient administration of assets is not considered.

16. In the Lima-Callao conurbation, 70 percent of districts have a city cadastre, but only half as many are complete and up to date. Of Peru's 26 main cities, only 45 percent have a city cadastre and 30 percent have a complete cadastre (personal communication from the National Urban Development director, June 2008).

17. Each local municipality manages a specific budget using transfers from the central government and its own resources, including property tax, which is justified to pay for municipal services. Poor municipalities do not have resources to offer services and, consequently, have no legitimacy for tax collection. This vicious circle is fed by opponents who typically use the nonpayment argument as a political platform.

18. The private domain includes land not for public use—such as arid wasteland, real estate belonging to ministries, and land confiscated from drug traffickers—that can be conveyed to private individuals.

19. Law 29151, Article 9, establishes that any divestment of property from the private domain of the state to the benefit of individuals must have as reference the commercial value of the land and be made according to the procedures and existing legal norms, because these assets belong to the nation.

20. In the past, expropriation could be justified in the "social interest," that is, benefiting specific groups. This practice justified many expropriations during the land reforms undertaken in the 1960s and 1970s. The reference to social interest, however, was removed in the 1990 constitution.

21. Road concessionaries highlight that some speculators organize groups to invade lands along the route of planned roads with the sole purpose of negotiating compensation. They argue that, therefore, the existing practice is sufficient and formal recognition of occupancy rights are not needed.

22. The National Public Registries System is managed by the National Superintendency of Public Registries (SUNARP) and comprises the Natural Persons Registry, the Juridical Persons Registry, the Property Registry, the Movable Goods Registry, and the Movable Guarantees Registry. SUNARP provides registration services through 58 decentralized registration offices and 23 windows (branch offices that act as front desks and receive requests for services that are processed in the main registration offices) throughout the country.

23. An empirical study based on a survey in 2007 showed that only 21 percent of the users willing to register could gather the documentation to present an application, and only 14 percent succeeded in obtaining the registrar's approval for registration (Gago 2007).

24. To prepare this mosaic, a specialist draws a polygon based on the actual recorded descriptions (metes and bounds) in property titles. This information is then digitized and, to the extent possible, linked to known physical landmarks that are based, for example, on satellite imagery. Because text descriptions were not drafted with measurements, the mosaic reflects the "legal truth" of registrations but does not necessarily match ground realities for which a separate, and more expensive, survey will be required. As a result, the cadastral certifications provided by the registry can serve to prove only what is recorded and the way it is recorded The mosaic now covers some 50 percent of the country, and experience so far suggests that it provides a cost-effective way of constructing a spatial reference that is a practical tool for the users. The exercise of matching records with ground realities (in those cases where the records are wrong) requires contracting surveyors, producing new maps, and initiating a court procedure for the rectification of the property records. That process is not being initiated by the registry and requires individual users to incur significant related expenses. As a result, the building of the mosaic provides a solution in those areas where overlapping rights are not recurrent (typically, urban areas where boundaries are well defined). However, in rural areas, although the mosaic is a useful tool, it still reflects a legal truth that can differ widely from what is found in the field.

25. Inefficiencies include (a) high costs of long-term residence under precarious conditions and possibly fees paid by settlers to informal developers, (b) costs incurred by governments for providing services to distant areas, and (c) externalities arising from unplanned cities for society at large.

26. The National Cadastre System Law was passed in 2004. It deals with registry issues and established a strategy and schemes to create and preserve an updated registry cadastre, including links between cadastre-generating bodies (that is, municipalities, titling agencies, and ministries managing land use restrictions or natural resources concessions) and the property registry itself. Such links would enable them to standardize criteria; share information; and determine the role of notaries, public and private practitioners, and other system parties. However, five years after the law was passed, no significant progress has been made, principally because of trouble involved in coordinating initiatives across organizations and insufficient technical and budget resources among local governments.

27. During systematic first-time registration, 34 percent of all registered property units were registered based on nondocumentary forms of evidence.

28. According to Article 13 of the Law of the Kyrgyz Republic on the Foundation of the State Guarantees for Gender Equality (March 2003, No. 60), amended by the State Guarantees of Equal Rights and Equal Opportunities for Men and Women (August 2008, No. 184), the right to land is equally reserved for persons of both sexes.

29. The resulting report is available at Gosregister, http://www.gosreg.kg, and at the National Statistics Committee. The efficiency of conducting land transactions also improved. Average processing time for sales transactions was reduced to 1.3 days by 2010.

30. Government Resolution 210 from September 18, 2010, cancelled the restriction on allocating any land to new individual housing in the main cities (including Bishkek) that had been in force for the past 5 years.

31. These include agricultural land (arable land, irrigated and dry land, perennial plantings, hay land, and pastures), land plots near the house, land plots of settlement areas, and land for commercial purposes.

32. The situation has changed since the report was written, with information on these and other transactions now publicly available and scheduled to be made available on the Web in 2011.

33. Since this document was written, promulgation of the Government resolution for a new uniform and open coordinate system (Kyrg 06) for all nonclassified survey purposes in October 2010 provides the basis for further improvements in access to spatial data. Digitization and georeferencing of all index maps planned for the two next years will create a more transparent cadastral database.

34. This information gap is being addressed with registration of municipal land that has been actively initiated in 2009.

35. As of April 30, 2009, a uniform fee for conducting a registration (less than US$4) has been adopted.

36. Activities started in 2010 to create a single enterprise to enable sustainable maintenance and development of the system of a cadastre and registration of the rights to immovable property. This would include provisions to finance the ongoing provision of central services with enterprise revenue and to rationalize local offices. It is hoped that the single enterprise will be operational by the end of 2011. The Second Land and Real Estate Registration Project is also supporting the development of an automated system of accounting; a new corporate governance framework for financial management; and international standards of audit, including an independent external audit once a single enterprise has been established.

37. Though most observers in Tanzania consider the 1999 Land Act and Village Land Act to be an acceptable basis for moving forward, opinions are quite divided between critics (Shivji 1998) and supporters (Alden-Wily 2003).

38. Tanzania is divided into 21 regions. In urban areas, 25 authorities include city, municipal, and town councils. Rural areas contain 106 administrative districts (district councils), 10,397 registered villages, and 97 designated township authorities.

39. By March 2011, the number of villages with a CVL (though not necessarily together with preparation of a land use plan) had increased to 6,616, demonstrating that it is possible to achieve rapid progress in some of these areas.

40. Although the approval process has been somewhat decentralized since then, there is still no clear justification why, with very few exceptions that are of limited practical relevance practice, any land transferred to large-scale agricultural investors must be expropriated first, an arrangement that makes direct agreements between

villagers and outsiders impossible. Other countries have found that focusing public efforts on providing technical and legal advice in the process and ensuring that certain minimum standards are met can be a desirable alternative. Comments on restrictions on transferability of village land are quite harsh without giving details on what they are and whether they are rational.

41. The government argues that implementing orderly land development schemes is easier if third-party interests are completely extinguished before any subsequent development is undertaken. This approach reflects a very paternalistic belief in which existing landowners will not be able to make appropriate use of the development opportunities brought about by changes in land use, for example, through joint ventures. An alternative, which might also allow addressing of the problems encountered in paying compensation, could be to speed up registration and to make transferability easier.

42. Following the writing of this text, some decentralization has taken place through the appointment of Assistant Commissioners in Zonal Offices who have been delegated some authority by the Commissioner of Lands.

43. After being a monarchy that recognized kinship, tenancy, and private tenure, the country nationalized land and redistributed it under a socialist regime (1974–91). That regime was replaced by a free market economy in which land remains public, but private holdings are recognized and encouraged.

44. For rural areas, see the Rural Land Administration Proclamation (No. 89/1997) and the Rural Land Administration and Land Use Proclamation (No. 456/2005) issued at the federal level; the Revised Amhara National Regional State Rural Land Administration and Use Proclamation (No. 133/2006); the Regulation for the Implementation of Proclamation 133/2006 (Regulation No. 51/2007); Oromia National Regional State Proclamation (No. 130/2007), Proclamation to Amend Proclamations 56/2002, 70/2003, 103/2005 of the Oromia Rural Land Administration and Utilization Proclamation; Southern Nations, Nationalities, and Peoples Regions Rural Land Administration and Utilization Proclamation (No. 110/2007); Tigray National Regional State, Rural Land Administration, and Utilization Proclamation (No. 97/2006); and Tigray Land Administration and Utilization Regulation (Regulation No. 37/2007). For urban areas, see Proclamation No. 80/1993 and the Lease Proclamation No. 272/2002.

45. The remaining regions (Afar, Benishangul-Gumuz, Gambella, Harar, and Somali) lack implementing legislation, making it difficult to formally recognize or enforce peasants' and pastoralists' rights. Afar is reported to have issued a rural land administration proclamation recently.

46. In theory, investors can pledge their use rights over the remaining lease period as collateral.

47. For instance, the SNNP land administration law (Proclamation No. 110/2007) provides that land rent among peasants can be for a duration of up to 5 years and for investors for a duration of up to 10 years, or rent may extend up to 25 years if the investor is cultivating perennial crops (Article 8). The Oromia Land Administration Law (Proclamation No. 130/2007) provides a duration of up to 3 years if the land is rented out to traditional farmers and up to 15 years for mechanized farming and also limits the land to be rented out to half of a peasant's landholding (Article 10).

48. The Lease Proclamation (No. 272/2002, Art. 12/2) states that urban land use may be changed only through a permit granted in writing by the appropriate body. Subsection 3 of the same article provides that the period of a lease for urban land, performance of payments, and tax rates are to be changed upon such conversion. This part seems intended to allow the government to capture a share of benefits arising from land use changes.

49. Article 13 of the Lease Proclamation (No. 272/2002) stipulates that any leasehold possessor can transfer or mortgage the right of leasehold.

50. These lower levels of government that receive mandates are the village (*kebele*), district (*woreda*), municipality, zone, and region.

51. See, for example, Article 5 of the Rural Land Administration and Land Use Proclamation No. 456/2005.

52. The typical fee for an average 75-square-meter house in Addis Ababa that would be valued at ETB 150,000 (US$12,000) is about ETB 1,000 (US$80), that is, 0.7 percent of the value of a typical house.

53. Normally, municipal officials determine a benchmark price for prime land in urban centers and then apply discount factors to other locations, mainly depending on the level of local infrastructure.

54. For a sample of parcels, open market values were between 20 and 60 times the lease, with permit fees being even lower (World Bank 2007).

55. Amhara has recently introduced an auction system to grant land to investors, but prices are still well below the market reference.

56. The total regional government revenue from urban land leases for the year ending May 2008 was more than ETB 2.6 billion (about US$156 million), as compared to a mere ETB 187 million (about US$11.2 million) from lease payments by investors for rural land use (Regional Government Revenue from Rural Land Use Fee and Urban Land Lease Fees [2007/2008], General Government Revenue, Consolidated Budget [2008/09]).

57. The first stage involves the issuance of textual holding certificates that identify neighbors. They do not include boundary descriptions that are to be provided by cadastral maps, which are to be generated in a second stage.

58. For example, landholding certificates in Oromia and SNNP provide no space for updating. Registers used in Amhara, Oromia, and Tigray provide spaces for transfer through inheritance or expropriation. Short-term transfers are not considered in the registers of any region.

59. The unambiguous demarcation of forestland further increases tenure insecurity and leads to frequent land conflicts.

60. Surveys undertaken in the context of LGAF implementation in Bandung, Depok, and Jakarta point toward 20 percent of land ownership by women.

61. Significantly more parcels are in the fiscal cadastre for purposes of taxation than are in the legal cadastre for determination of property rights.

REFERENCES

Alden-Wily, L. 2003. "Community-Based Land Tenure Management: Questions and Answers about Tanzania's New Village Land Act, 1999." IIED Issues Paper 120, International Institute for Environment and Development, London.

Gago, H. 2007. *El Registro Público como Problema para Democratizar la Propiedad*. Lima: United Nations Development Programme for Latin America.

Garcia, A. 2007. "El Síndrome del Perro del Hortelano: Poner en Valor los Recursos no Utilizados." *El Comercio.* October 28, page 4.

Personal Communication from the National Urban Development director, June 2008.

Shivji, I. 1998. *Not Yet Democracy: Reforming Land Tenure in Tanzania*. London: International Institute for Environment and Development.

World Bank. 2007. "The Challenge of Urbanization in Ethiopia: Implications for Growth and Poverty Alleviation." World Bank, Water and Urban Development Unit I, Africa Region, Washington, DC.

CHAPTER FIVE

Conclusion and Next Steps

This chapter examines how well the pilot application of the Land Governance Assessment Framework (LGAF) in five countries (Ethiopia, Indonesia, the Kyrgyz Republic, Peru, and Tanzania) lived up to expectations. It assesses the usefulness of the framework and the scope for using it as one input—to be developed and improved in the course of implementation—into broader efforts to improve land governance. These would not only explore land governance in other countries, but also establish ways of measuring it on a continuing basis.

METHODOLOGICAL AND PROCESS LESSONS FROM THE PILOT

A key underlying hypothesis for the framework was that a sector-specific approach to governance has many advantages and that, the differences in historical context notwithstanding, a framework that is identical across countries will have many benefits. Among the benefits are the ability to systematically identify good practice in specific countries (though not necessarily to obtain a country score), to identify global best practice in specific areas, and to point toward good practice in policy reform. The pilot cases support this hypothesis. They demonstrate that a structured diagnostic review of the land administration system in a given country can be performed without imposing value judgments. Though much learning was involved, the pilots also helped refine the framework and provided lessons regarding implementation. Some refinements are already reflected in the LGAF. Although not all elements are equally relevant everywhere, the general feeling is that coverage is broad enough (without becoming too complex), and the framework is of sufficient scope, to adapt to country-specific conditions in the inception stage. Thus, the LGAF is considered to be ready for rollout to other countries with the expectation of producing useful results.

A key decision that differentiates the LGAF from other tools such as Public Expenditure and Financial Accountability (PEFA) is the strong emphasis on the involvement of local experts and users who interact with the land system in a wide range of contexts. This participation has proved to be critical to draw on the range of required experience to document and identify areas for policy action. At the same time, two areas for improvement of the tool can be identified. First, the way and extent to which government was involved in the process lacked coherence, something that could affect the extent to which policy recommendations will be acted upon. Although the wide range of potential arrangements makes it difficult to supply general recommendations across countries, desirable elements are a general agreement with government that would include access to whatever data are available, as well as an arrangement for obtaining official comments and disseminating results through a joint workshop and for allowing the country coordinator to control the extent of government officials' involvement.[1] For the conduct of assessments as an input to other global initiatives in a country context, a formal mandate under this umbrella could be very useful. Second, as experience on implementation of the LGAF accumulates, ensuring that country coordinators have access to procedural and substantive lessons from other countries will be important to make the process as effective as possible and to prevent costly learning by trial and error. To that end, a detailed LGAF Implementation Manual has been written, providing all the procedural material, and will greatly facilitate implementation. Workshops with country coordinators could also be organized before beginning the work, and a global coordinator could be involved throughout the process and in dissemination workshops.

The use of an identical structure for a heterogeneous set of countries would make it possible to identify good practice that could potentially be transferred across countries, as well as to identify areas that are problematic and warrant more analytical efforts. Indeed, results suggest that, even in the pilots, many lessons and good practices could be transferred across countries in each of the five main areas. These findings are critical for providing feedback to the policy dialogue, such as to show that innovative solutions are available, and could in turn provide the basis for a vigorous South-South exchange of experience.[2]

KEY SUBSTANTIVE AREAS FOR EXPANSION OF THE LGAF

The LGAF provides an exhaustive diagnostic assessment of the most relevant land governance issues common to most developing countries. However, to deal with specific country conditions or emerging themes, implementers could extend the focus beyond the standard LGAF that was piloted. For instance, an example of an emerging theme is the rising global interest in land noted by a number of recent high-profile initiatives, such as the Voluntary Guidelines of the Food and Agriculture Organization of the United Nations and the African Union's Framework and Guidelines on Land Policy, and high levels of interest from the private sector. These programs require investments to improve infrastructure, to manage risks, and to strengthen and monitor tenure security. The LGAF provides a framework that can be applied to the country context to make contributions in this respect.

These programs have led the LGAF country pilots team to envision adding specific indicators to an otherwise standard LGAF to explore in more depth such particular issues or themes. For instance, within the framework of a parallel global study undertaken by some members of the LGAF team (see Deininger et al. 2011), a module of 16 additional indicators was designed to assess governance regarding large-scale land acquisition. These indicators form an optional module that can be added to a standard LGAF (see table 5.1 for a list of these 16 indicators).[3] Similarly, other modules could be developed to implement an expanded LGAF that focuses on a particular sector or an important issue critical to land governance. An LGAF module on forestry is currently being drafted. Other topics that could be covered include financial sector management, municipal finance, natural resources management, gender and access to land, climate change, and more, all of which have important links to land governance. For instance, land policy and administration can play a key role in planning adaptation to climate change in the developing world.[4]

WHERE SHOULD THE LGAF GO FROM HERE?

In the five studied countries, the LGAF was used to identify gaps in policy and the way institutions function or responsibilities between institutions are assigned. A framework that ascertains issues in a structured way allows the use of good practice that has been identified in one country setting to help identify options for policy reform in another. Being able to draw lessons from solutions to seemingly difficult policy areas in a variety of contexts can help policy reforms gain momentum. If applied in a way that, from the beginning, draws on existing expertise and broad participation by relevant stakeholders (including governments), the LGAF can help to broaden not only the range of issues to be covered in such a review, but also the relevance of the resulting analysis and the credibility of resulting recommendations for policy or further study. The proposed modular approach—that is, adding a standardized module of additional indicators to the core set of common indicators—also makes the tool useful for combining tailored diagnoses within a synoptic assessment of land governance. Developing such modules in the future will make the

Table 5.1	Dimensions Added to the Standard LGAF to Study Land Governance in the Context of Large-Scale Acquisitions of Agricultural Land

Additional dimensions	Topic
1	Most forestland is mapped and rights are registered.
2	Land acquisition generates few conflicts, and these are addressed expeditiously and transparently.
3	Land use restrictions on rural land parcels can generally be identified.
4	Public institutions involved in land acquisition operate in a clear and consistent manner.
5	Incentives for investors are clear, transparent, and consistent.
6	Benefit-sharing mechanisms regarding investments in agriculture (food crops, biofuels, forestry, livestock, and game farm and conservation) are regularly used and transparently applied.
7	There are direct and transparent negotiations between right holders and investors.
8	Sufficient information is required from investors to assess the desirability of projects on public or communal land.
9	For cases of land acquisition on public or community land, investors provide the required information, and this information is publicly available.
10	Contractual provisions regarding acquisition of land from communities or the public are required by law to explicitly mention the way in which benefits and risks will be shared.
11	The procedure to obtain approval for a project where it is required is reasonably short.
12	Social requirements for large-scale investments in agriculture are clearly defined and implemented.
13	Environmental requirements for large-scale investments in agriculture are clearly defined and implemented.
14	For transfers of public or community lands, public institutions have procedures in place to identify and select economically, environmentally, and socially beneficial investments and to implement these effectively.
15	Compliance with safeguards related to investment in agriculture is checked.
16	There are avenues to lodge complaints if agricultural investors do not comply with requirements.

LGAF a flexible tool to meet the demand for analysis of country-specific topics without neglecting a core assessment of land governance.

Beyond this function, two other areas might be addressed jointly by development partners. First, the LGAF can provide a basis to monitor discrete (rule-based) indicators of policy reform and, in doing so, provide an opportunity for a broad-based coalition of actors (including nongovernmental organizations, the private sector, and academics) to monitor the extent to which recommendations are followed through on. In fact, in Peru, panel members suggested that putting in place a structure to provide such follow-up would be possible with modest resources. Discussions along that line are ongoing. This function for the LGAF is very similar to that of the land observatories that have already been established in various contexts, and the framework could build on that structure to work toward establishing broad-based land working groups at the national level. Such a group could provide regular input into national forums, such as the Comprehensive Africa Agriculture Development Programme roundtables to provide specific operational guidance to policy. This group could be linked to agreement on specific steps and report on progress made toward improving land governance in response to multilateral initiatives such as that of the African Union or of other institutions.

Second, beyond the discrete indicators, the LGAF points to a number of areas that change relatively quickly and in which the design of quantitative indicators to monitor land governance on a more frequent basis will thus be useful. Although more work will be needed to agree on the specific definition of variables, the LGAF experience suggests that key areas of concern include (a) the coverage of the land administration system (that is, the extent to which primary or secondary rights of groups or individuals are recorded) and the extent to which different types of transfers are registered, with particular attention to women; (b) the amount of land tax revenue that is raised; (c) the total area of public or private land that is mapped with publicly available information; (d) the number of expropriations and the modalities for compensation (including amounts and delays in receipt of payment); and (e) the number of conflicts of different types entering the formal system. The fact that each of these indicators is related to one or more core areas of the land administration system suggests that the collection and publication of these indicators on a regular basis, and in a way that can be easily disaggregated by administrative units,[5] should be routine in any land administration system and should be integrated in future donor support in the land area.

In fact, addressing the two elements, that is, monitoring discrete measures of policy and designing specific quantitative indicators, would provide the basis for a more results-based way of providing support to the land sector that could help increase accountability at the national level. It would also help with the sharing of experience and collaboration across countries to effectively address some of the challenges in trying to improve land governance.

NOTES

1. In a number of instances during the pilot, involvement of midlevel government officials unwilling to admit to shortcomings in the way the system operated made it impossible for the panel to come to a consensus view. If there is a danger of this happening, a useful approach would probably be to have the panel present a user view of the system and to gather consolidated government comments thereafter but before a public workshop is held.

2. The LGAF allows the use of case studies that demonstrate the feasibility of specific reforms and changes in agreed-upon indicators over time, rather than using the computation of an abstract land governance score for comparison across countries.

3. This augmented LGAF was used as a basis for an analysis of land governance in 14 countries by local experts, but the application of the full LGAF methodology was not required.

4. A publication by the Food and Agriculture Organization of the United Nations recently observed: "Although the linkages between climate change and land tenure are complex and indirect, the effects of climate change and variability are felt through changes in natural ecosystems, land capability and land use systems. Increasingly, these changes will place diminishing supplies of land under greater pressure, for both productive use and human settlement. As a result land issues and policies should be key considerations for adaptation planning, so as to strengthen land tenure and management arrangements in at risk environments, and secure supplies and access arrangements for land for resettlement and changing livelihood demands" (FAO 2008, 4).

5. There are indeed wide variations of these indicators across locations.

REFERENCES

Deininger, K., D. Byerlee, J. Lindsay, A. Norton, H. Selod, and M. Stickler. 2011. *Rising Global Interest in Farmland: Can It Yield Sustainable and Equitable Benefits?* Washington, DC: World Bank.

FAO (Food and Agriculture Organization of the United Nations). 2008. "Climate Change, Bioenergy, and Land Tenure." Technical Background Document HLC/08/BAK/9, FAO, Rome.

INDEX

Boxes, figures, notes, and tables are indicated with *b*, *f*, *n*, and *t* following the page number.

C

cadastre systems
    development of, 65, 128*n*36
    mapping and, 102–3, 120, 123
    property registry and, 68, 127*n*26
    in urban areas, 106–7, 126*n*16
capacity-building efforts, 107, 123
children, rights recognition for, 28–29
city civil squads (*rondas urbanas*), 66
civil society groups, 20
Clearance Order Appeals
    Commission, 96
climate change, 11, 14
COFOPRI. *See* Commission for the
    Formalization of Informal
    Property
collateral, land as
    disincentive to using, 73
    permits and, 84
    recognition of rights and, 28
collective farms, 68
colonos (indigenous group), 59, 67
Commissioner of Lands, 88
Commission for the Formalization of
    Informal Property (Organismo
    de la Formalización de la
    Propiedad Informal), 55, 61,
    65–66, 67
Commonwealth of Independent
    States, 68
community rights, recognition of,
    59–60, 67
Comprehensive Africa Agriculture
    Development Programme, 137
comuneros (indigenous group), 59
condominium holdings, 95, 116
Condominium Proclamation No.
    370/2003 (Ethiopia), 95
conflict management. *See* dispute
    resolution
consensus rating systems, 39
corruption
    land information and, 76
    Land Redistribution Fund and, 75
    in land sector, 12, 13–14, 22*n*2
    public land allocation and, 34
    zoning regulations and, 31
country coordinators, 49

Country Policy and Institutional
    Assessment, 16, 23*n*10
country reports from expert panels, 48
courts of elders (*aksakal courts*), 77
credit, access to, 14
customary laws, 66, 107, 117, 122

D

decentralization
    in Ethiopia, 107
    in Indonesia, 8, 107, 117, 123
    in Kyrgyz Republic, 73–74, 78
    in Peru, 54–55, 60, 67–68
    in Tanzania, 85, 88–89, 129*n*42
decision-making process, equity in,
    30–31
deeds systems, 36*n*6
deforestation, 15, 59
Department for International
    Development (U.K.), 50*n*1
developing countries
    land governance and, 15, 134
    recognition of rights in, 29
Development Agency (France), 19
development permits. *See* building and
    development permits
dispute resolution
    conflicts, numbers of, 137
    in Ethiopia, 104, 107
    expert panels and, 48
    in Indonesia, 121, 124
    in Kyrgyz Republic, 77
    Land Governance Assessment
        Framework and, 2, 28, 35–36
    in Peru, 66
    in Tanzania, 86–87, 90
Doing Business indicators (World
    Bank), 19–20, 23*n*15

E

Economic Commission of Africa, 49
Economy, Industry and Employment
    Ministry (France), 19
enforcement of land rights. *See* rights
    enforcement and recognition
equity in decision-making process,
    30–31
Ethiopia, 53, 90–107

I

IFAD. *See* International Fund for
    Agricultural Development
IMF (International Monetary Fund),
    50*n*1
India, bribes in, 13
Indonesia, 53, 107–24
    decentralization in, 8, 107, 117, 123
    dispute resolution in, 121, 124
    institutional framework in, 117, 122
    Land Governance Assessment
        Framework in, 22
    land information in, 120–21, 123–24
    land use planning and taxation in,
        117–19, 123
    policy recommendations for, 7–9,
        121–24
    public land management in,
        119–20, 123
    rights recognition in, 108–16, 121–22
    rural areas in, 112–15*b*
    service delivery in, 124
    spatial planning in, 122–23
    tenure typology in, 108, 109–15*t*
    urban areas in, 109–11*t*, 116, 118
    women's land rights in, 116
information on land. *See* land
    information
inheritance rights, 7, 84, 94, 105
institutional frameworks
    in Ethiopia, 96–97
    in Indonesia, 117, 122
    in Kyrgyz Republic, 73–74
    Land Governance Assessment
        Framework and, 2, 28–31
    in Peru, 60–61
    in Tanzania, 84, 88
Inter-American Alliance for Real
    Property Rights, 16
International Development
    Association, 23*n*10
International Finance Corporation,
    23*n*12
International Food Policy Research
    Institute, 9
International Fund for Agricultural
    Development (IFAD), 9, 16,
    23*n*10

International Monetary Fund (IMF),
    50*n*1
International Property Rights Index,
    21, 23*n*15

J

Jakarta (Indonesia)
    land information in, 120
    land use planning in, 117
joint ventures, 129*n*41
Justice and Constitutional Affairs
    Ministry (Tanzania), 87

K

Kenya
    businesses in, 22*n*3
    land-related fraud in, 13
Knack, S., 22*n*1
Kyrgyz Land Information System, 78
Kyrgyz Republic, 53, 68–78
    decentralization in, 73–74, 78
    dispute resolution in, 77
    government revenues in, 78
    information sharing in, 78
    institutional framework in, 73–74
    Land Governance Assessment
        Framework in, 22
    land information in, 76, 128*n*33
    land redistribution in, 77–78
    land use planning and taxation in, 74
    policy recommendations for, 4–5,
        77–78
    public land management in, 75
    rights recognition in, 69–73
    tenure typology for, 69, 70–72*t*
    women's land rights in, 69, 128*n*28

L

Land Acquisition Act (Tanzania), 89
Land Act (LA, Tanzania), 5, 78, 83,
    128*n*37
Land Administration Project
    (Indonesia), 116
Land Code (Kyrgyz Republic), 75
land courts, 86
Land Governance Assessment
    Framework (LGAF). *See also*
    land governance frameworks

Peru, 53–68
    decentralization in, 54–55, 60, 67–68
    demand for land in, 54
    dispute resolution in, 66
    institutional framework for, 60–61
    land administration, equity in, 66–67
    Land Governance Assessment
        Framework in, 22, 137
    land information in, 64–65, 127*n*24
    land policy achievements in, 68
    land use planning and taxation in,
        61–62, 126*n*15
    natural resources in, 126*n*13
    policy recommendations for, 3–4,
        66–68
    rights recognition in, 55–60
    rural areas, property rights in, 67
    state-owned lands in, 62–64, 63*b*
    tenure typology for, 55, 56–58*t*
    urban areas in, 54, 67
    women's land rights in, 55
political power, land governance and,
    12, 20–21
polygamy, 95, 105
poverty and the poor
    access to land and, 27
    dispute resolution and, 124
    housing and, 67
    land use planning and, 89
    tax breaks and, 68
private sector, community groups
    and, 60
Public Expenditure and Financial
    Accountability (PEFA), 39–40,
    46, 50–51*n*1, 134
public land management
    in Ethiopia, 100–101
    in Indonesia, 119–20, 123
    in Kyrgyz Republic, 75
    Land Governance Assessment
        Framework and, 2, 28, 32–34
    in Tanzania, 85–86
public-private partnerships, 119
public sector. *See also* public land
    management
    clarity of institutional mandates
        in, 30
    role of, 12

R
recognition of land rights. *See* rights
    enforcement and recognition
registration of land rights. *See also* land
    information
    currency of, 46
    enforcement and, 29, 116
    as land management
        incentive, 31
    mapping and, 65, 117, 120
    mechanisms for, 29–30
    public information and, 34–35
    standardization of, 68
    title registration, 34
rezoning, 31–32, 33
ribereños (indigenous group), 59
rights enforcement and recognition
    in Ethiopia, 90–95
    in Indonesia, 108–16, 121–22
    in Kyrgyz Republic, 69–73
    Land Governance Assessment
        Framework and, 29
    in Peru, 55–60
    in Tanzania, 78–83
rights-of-way, negotiating of, 60
risk mitigation, 50*b*
road construction companies, 64,
    127*n*21
rural areas
    auctions in, 100
    boundary disputes in, 65
    emigration from, 69
    expert panels and, 48
    expropriation in, 85
    informality in, 106
    land productivity in, 14, 59
    land purchasing in, 73
    land registration in, 88–89,
        102, 107
    land tenure in, 90, 94, 112–15*b*
    land use planning in, 89
    proofs of credit in, 125*n*7
    registered village land in, 83
    rights recognition in, 55, 67
    tax collection in, 99
    women's land ownership in, 69,
        97, 105
Rural Development Policy, 89

land information and, 76
of land use restrictions, 31
in land valuation and tax
collection, 32
in public land management, 33,
34, 47
rights recognition and, 29, 30
service delivery and, 124

U

United Nations Human Settlements
Program (UN-Habitat), 9,
16, 17b
United States Agency for International
Development (USAID), 16
urban areas. *See also* peri-urban areas
cadastre systems in, 106–7
condominium holdings in, 95
expert panels and, 48
informality in, 84–85, 103,
106, 118
land productivity in, 14
land registry in, 88–89
land tenure in, 17b, 109–11t
land use planning in, 74, 89, 97–98,
105, 128n30
property rights in, 67, 127n25
reserved land in, 83
rights recognition in, 55, 59, 116
squatting in, 84
tax collection in, 74, 99
Urban Land Lease Holding
Proclamation No. 272/2002
(Ethiopia), 94, 129–30nn48–49
usufruct rights certificates, 102

V

Village Land Act (VLA, Tanzania), 5,
78, 83, 128n37

W

wildlife reserves, 100
women. *See also* women's land rights
dispute resolution and, 77
land tenure and, 14, 46
rights recognition for, 28–29
rural areas, land ownership in, 69,
97, 105
women's land rights
in Ethiopia, 102, 105
in Indonesia, 116
in Kyrgyz Republic, 69, 128n28
in Peru, 55
in Tanzania, 84, 88, 95
World Bank
on access to land, 22n3
experts from, 49
land governance and, 9, 16, 19, 22n8,
23n10, 23n15
land registration and, 69
Public Expenditure and Financial
Accountability and, 50n1
World Economic Forum, 23n15
Worldwide Governance Indicators 2006
(World Bank), 22n8

Y

Yabello Sanctuary, 100

Z

zoning. *See* rezoning